D0066121

Praise for *Knit Purl Pray*

Whether you're a knitter or not, *Knit Purl Pray* is filled with life vignettes, knitting together the threads of daily creativity and that tie with our Lord.

Debbie Macomber

#1 *New York Times* best-selling author

Knit Purl Pray sounds only for knitters in spite of the line "52 Devotions for the Creative Soul." Knitting is a struggle for me, but I love to crochet. But Lisa has done a magnificent job of using her passion for knitting to offer all of us who do creative things—be it with yarn, fabric, paint, clay, wood, words, or metal—other views on how we can worship our Lord with what we do. How we can reach out to others who enjoy our same craft or make something for someone else, be it for beauty's sake or daily use. We can share our joy, our skills, our love, and our laughter—honoring our Lord God who gave us all gifts to serve Him and His family. *Knit Purl Pray* is a keeper to be enjoyed repeatedly and shared, like a hug from Lisa.

Lauraine Snelling, award-winning, best-selling author

of more than 80 books, including *An Untamed Heart*

knit purl pray

52
*Devotions
for the
Creative Soul*

LISA
BOGART

WORTHY®
Inspired

Copyright © 2015 by Lisa Bogart

ISBN 978-1-61795-576-1

Published by Worthy Inspired, an imprint of Worthy Publishing Group,
a division of Worthy Media, Inc., One Franklin Park, 6100 Tower Circle,
Suite 210, Franklin, TN 37067.

Bogart, Lisa, 1960-
  Knit, purl, pray : 52 devotions for the creative soul / Lisa Bogart.
    pages cm
  Includes bibliographical references and index.
  ISBN 978-1-61795-576-1 (hard cover : alk. paper)
  1. Knitters (Persons)—Prayers and devotions. 2. Knitting. 3. Christian
women—Religious life. I. Title.
  BV4596.N44B63 2015
  242'.68—dc23
                            2015022516

Unless indicated otherwise, Scripture is taken from THE HOLY BIBLE, NEW
INTERNATIONAL VERSION®, NIV® Copyright © 1973, 1978, 1984, 2011 by
Biblica, Inc.® Used by permission. All rights reserved worldwide.

Scripture references marked GW are from the Holy Bible. GOD'S WORD®, ©
1995 God's Word to the Nations. Used by permission of Baker Publishing Group.

Scripture quotations marked MSG are taken from The Message. Copyright ©
1993, 1994, 1995, 1996, 2000, 2001, 2002. Used by permission of NavPress
Publishing Group.

All rights reserved. No part of this publication may be reproduced, stored in
a retrieval system, or transmitted in any form or by any means—electronic,
mechanical, photocopy, recording, scanning, or other—except for brief quotations
in critical reviews or articles, without the prior written permission of the publisher.

Cover Design by Jeffery Jansen / Aesthetic Soup
Illustrations by: Diane Labombarbe and Christine-Krahl / iStock.com

Printed in the United States of America

1 2 3 4 5 6—LBM—19 18 17 16 15

Contents

Introduction   9

1. Sticks and String   11
2. Welcome!   13
3. The Kitchener Stitch   15
4. Hidden Treasures   17
5. Lacework   19
6. Head to Toe   22
7. Weighing In   24
8. Biblical Knitter   26
9. The Fabric of Life   28
10. Tuesday Night Knits   30
11. Woolen Prayers   32
12. Lifelines   34
13. What Is It?   36
14. Marked by Love   39
15. Threads of History   42
16. Raglan Construction   44
17. Lessons from My Knit Bag   47
18. Swatches   49
19. Follow the Directions   51

20. Picture Perfect   53

21. The Search   55

22. Monkey Mind   57

23. The LYS (Local Yarn Shop)   59

24. Fresh Eyes   62

25. The Selfish Knitter   64

26. Yarn overs   67

27. Gifts to Share   69

28. Metal or Bamboo   71

29. Bundled Up   74

30. Multitasking   76

31. Happy Hobbies   78

32. The Learning Curve   81

33. Knitting Lesson   84

34. Mistakes   87

35. Novelty Yarns   89

36. Don't Help Me   91

37. Goldilocks   94

38. Full-Sized Love   97

39. Comfort for the Furry   100

40. Superpowers   102

41. Knit for Marie   104

42. Baby Sweaters   106

43. Heating Up and Making Changes   108

44. Nature's Patterns   111

45. Weaving in the Ends   113

46. Knit Your Bit   115

47. Progress on the Needles   118

48. Darn It!   120

49. Thanks, Mom   123

50. Wise Women   125

51. I Speak Knittish   128

52. Passion!   130

Patterns

The Slouchy Beehive Hat   133

Coffee Cup Cozies   137

Introduction

We knitters have a language all our own. We have a short hand in our conversations others find mysterious. We talk about decreasing and it's a good thing. We can slip, slip, knit and not lose a stitch. Even when we are practicing our craft, we appear a little different. Double-pointed needles are fascinating to watch in the hands of a knitter. We are a special group.

This book contains 52 devotions that speak your language. Many knitters love the solitude of time with needles and fiber. In that quiet time I looked for and found knitting connecting to my faith. You may already have a little quiet time carved out for knitting, but now you can add a quick read to give yourself a point to ponder while you are working.

You can literally open this book to any page and find an ah-ha moment. *Or* you can read them slowly in order. However you choose to read these thoughts hopefully you will have a moment of insight that brings you a little deeper into your faith. At the very least you will know there is another knitter like yourself who wonders, *How did my stash get so big?* From silly to serious I hope you will enjoy reading these faith knit thoughts.

Sticks and String

*And this is my prayer: that your love may abound more
and more in knowledge and depth of insight,
so that you may be able to discern what is best
and may be pure and blameless for the day of Christ.*

Philippians 1:9-10

Why do we play with sticks and string when so many other chores scream for our attention? Do you ever feel guilty about "wasting your time" knitting? I'll confess sometimes I'd rather knit than do just about anything else. It's hard to stop—one more row, one more pattern repeat. But chores beckon and work fills my desk. So between piles of dirty dishes in the sink and loads of laundry, I squeeze in time to make a few stitches. I actually set a timer since I know I'd rather knit than clean.

Why pause to knit? Escape! And I love the peace and quiet; knitting offers the perfect time for reflection. In this quiet frame of mind, my thoughts slow down and my muscles relax. I bet you enjoy the respite knitting gives too. This collection

of devotions offers a nugget to read so the heart can ponder while the fingers glide through stitch after stitch.

We knitters are patient people. We take the time to make socks rather than buy a pair. We see a scarf in the store and know we can make it better. We play with patterns. We collect yarn. We decide on colors. This hobby can consume lots of time and energy. And many of us use our knitting as a meditative time of the day. Knitting is a way to pause and think outside yourself, or a time to look within and find deeper meaning.

I'm inviting you to pick up this book of devotions now and then when you knit. I will offer you a little something to think about while you work on your current project. You may find a smile of recognition or a gentle conviction but always a look toward the heavens.

Grab this moment as your own. Enjoy the freedom to pause and find new insights into everyday ideas. This is time well spent; try not to worry about other pressing errands and chores. Have fun with your sticks and string and let your mind wander to heavenly things.

- -

Dear Father, I love quiet time with You!
And knitting while we have a moment alone is
such a bonus. Peace, yarn and You!
I'm a happy knitter! Amen

Welcome!

Do not forget to show hospitality to strangers,
for by so doing some people have shown hospitality
to angels without knowing it.

Hebrews 13:2

It was time for the knit shop to close. We were all packing up from Thursday Night Knitting when Linda said, "Thank you all for knitting with me. I look forward to this every week. I am so glad you all like to knit." I laughed, "I feel the same way. This is my favorite night of the week! I'm glad I found you." All the ladies nodded in agreement. We unanimously loved our weekly gathering.

This was a new knit group for me. I'd only lived in the area for six months. But from the very first night I walked into the lovely little shop, they were welcoming to me. I know this is not true of every group. It took a little searching to find a place where I could pull out my knitting and feel at home. However it just seems to me that knitters are quick to pull in new members. It starts with talking about craft, and soon enough we are sharing a little more and a little more of ourselves with each other.

The welcoming spirit of the knit group is a good reminder for me to bring that same hospitality feeling to all my interactions. Smiling at passersby as I walk on the street. Using my "pleases and thank yous" when people wait on me at the grocery store and other errands. Taking the time to stop what I'm doing, make eye contact, and listen to my family when they need to talk. Little ways to bring the pleasantness of knit night into the rest of my week. And then of course, grabbing my needles to go play with my friends and recharge with another knit night!

- -

Dear Father, thank You for the coziness
of a friendly gathering. Help me infuse the rest
of my week with those positive feelings.
Help me remember I can be kind and open
wherever I go. Amen

The Kitchener Stitch

If my people, who are called by my name, will humble
themselves and pray and seek my face and turn from
their wicked ways, then I will hear from heaven,
and I will forgive their sin and will heal their land.

2 Chronicles 7:14

The Kitchener stitch is used when you want the seam or join of your project to be invisible. It's most often used for grafting the toes of a sock together. A nifty technique but it's tricky. There may be only a dozen stitches to finish a sock, but it takes all my concentration to get right.

Often my knitting has vast rows of nothing exciting going on. So I let my mind wander. I make to-do lists in my head. I plan the errands of my day. I think of friends and family far away. I watch TV. I do a lot more than attend to the knitting in my hands. But it all comes to a full stop when I do the Kitchener stitch.

I am sure to loose my place and miss a stitch if I let my mind wander. To complete the task, I have to be in the moment. I can't veg-out and wander off mentally.

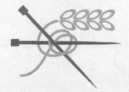

But it's easy to get distracted. It happens to me all the time. Attending a business meeting. Driving to work. Drifting off during a sermon. Chatting on a long phone conversation. I don't mean to but I disconnect.

Loosing my focus during prayer makes me feel guilty. I should be in the moment then. I am in the very presence of God. I am having an intimate conversation. There is no honor in wondering, *What's for dinner?* This all use to bother me very much until I realized I could talk with God in prayer more often.

I cling to the power of short prayer. A little prayer often goes a long way for keeping me connected to God. This is why I keep me prayers short and often. I do have a quiet time, but it's only the quick beginning to my day. Rather, I pray in short bursts throughout the day. I concentrate for the time it takes to praise, to plead, or to thank. Then I move on. Like working the Kitchener stitch, my prayers are short and concentrated.

- -

Dear Father, even in the rush of my day today,
keep me connected to You in prayer. Amen

Hidden Treasures

*But when you give to the needy, do not let your left hand
know what your right hand is doing, so that
your giving may be in secret. Then your Father,
who sees what is done in secret, will reward you.*

Matthew 6:3-4

I love to knit socks. I've made so many pair I've lost count. Today I pulled on my socks, put on my shoes, and realized my hand-knit beauties were covered up and no one could admire my lovely work. It didn't make me sad; in fact I was thinking what a cool little secret I had on my feet at this very moment. I have crazy socks on, hand-knit with expertise. It's taken me a while to enjoy hiding my knitting.

Most often no one ever sees the socks I make. Sure the people who get them are impressed for a little while, but eventually the socks are worn through and discarded. Should I cry over this? No, it's a cool gift to give someone, a secret something that makes them feel special. I like the undercover nature of socks. Not everyone can see the treat I lavished on someone else. It keeps me humble to know there is just one person who loves that pair of socks.

All my sock musing made me think about the verse of the right hand not knowing what the left hand is doing. And I wondered if it applied here. Do I knit the socks so I can feel cool, or do I knit them to surprise someone else? I like to think it's the surprise of giving someone a treat, but sometimes it's pride. I want the person to know about my amazing knit skills. I want them to be impressed. Like when someone watches me work on double-pointed needles. It just looks so impressively complicated, though with practice it becomes easier.

So I am trying to shift my focus. These days when I knit a pair of socks, I think about the person they are for and pray for them as I work. The hidden little gift of love will be just for them. I will send it with the hope they enjoy the secret fun of having hand-knit socks. And when the socks are worn through, I hope I'm ready to make another secret pair.

- -

Dear Father, let me rest in the secret
of a job well done for You. Amen

Lacework

"For I know the plans I have for you,"
declares the LORD, "plans to prosper you and
not to harm you, plans to give you hope and a future.
Then you will call on me and come
and pray to me, and I will listen to you.
You will seek me and find me when you
seek me with all your heart."

Jeremiah 29:11-13

I did it. I attempted a lace project. I have long been intimidated by lace, but it's so beautiful I wanted to give it a try. I started out simple with the leg of a sock: six stitches in the pattern repeat and only four rows in the design. Turns out, lace is great fun. It definitely kept me on my toes and challenged me.

I was still nervous working on my socks. I proceeded slowly to minimize mistakes. Troubleshooting a misstep in lace was hard for me. I could see a problem, but the only fix seemed to be ripping back. So I watched what I was doing very carefully.

Lace is full K2tog (knit 2 stitches together) to decrease and YO (yarn over) to increase. As well as S1 (slip one stitch) and PSSO (pass slip stich over worked stitch). All those increases and decreases are what make the holes. If you follow the pattern, the holes are formed in the right places and a pleasing design emerges. If you put the YOs and K2togs in the wrong places, there is no pretty pattern.

Paying attention to the details, I realized that over the space of one row no matter how many K2togs or YOs I did the number of stitches in the row remained constant. I wasn't loosing or gaining stitches; I was forming lace. So exciting to watch it grow on my needles.

I did finally get into the rhythm of my sock project and could knit along without checking the chart every single row. I started thinking about all those increases and decreases. It reminded me of how God seems to work in my life.

He takes things away (K2tog), and He gives blessings (yarn overs). But sometimes I can't see the whole pattern. I get frustrated not knowing why something is being taken away. Then by the time things are done (at the end of the row), there is a yarn over of blessing somewhere that has increased my life. I don't like the discipline of things being removed from me, but I am beginning to see it is necessary. It takes both increases and decreases for a pleasing pattern.

It took me a week to finish one lace cuff on that first sock. I ripped back several times to get it right. I had tried something hard and was rewarded with a glimpse of blessing. I am watched over by a God who loves me, One who has a plan for me. I receive both discipline and blessing in my life.

– –

Dear Father, I appreciate the blessings You pour in my life. Help me to see the things You withhold are equally a blessing to me. Amen

Head to Toe

Do you not know that in a race all the runners run,
but only one gets the prize? Run in such a way as to get
the prize. Everyone who competes in the games goes
into strict training. They do it to get a crown that will not last,
but we do it to get a crown that will last forever.

1 Corinthians 9:24-25

I put on hand-knit socks. I buttoned a cardigan. I pulled on fingerless mitts. I slipped a scarf around my neck and put a hat on my head. I was ready for an autumn walk. Then I laughed when I realized I was covered in yarn. Head to toe I was warm and toasty with merino and cashmere. I enjoy wearing the things I knit.

I admired my handiwork. Cables twisting up the front of my sweater. I remember the mystery of cables. I was surprised to learn they were relatively easy, just knitting the stitches out of order. I wiggled my toes. I remem-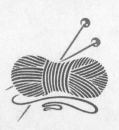ber thinking socks were beyond my knitting expertise. I was scared to even attempt them. Who knew they are just a tube that bends in the middle? I've learned so much through decades of knitting. Looking over my garments,

I felt wrapped in more then warmth. I felt accomplishment. I didn't realize what a stockpile of creations I had. Sometimes it's a good idea to take a look at how far you've come.

It's a good idea to take a look at how my Christian walk is going as well. I have been on this journey for years and have learned a lot. But to rest in the knowledge I have so far is to miss out on new facets of faith. I want to move toward a richer understanding and belief. Just as I learn new knit tricks and tips from the community I know, staying connecting to the faith community I will learn more about the God I love. Staying close to God in prayer is another way to grow in faith.

There is so much to discover. Sometimes I have to learn a faith lesson a second and even third or fourth time. And that is why I can't rest on my insights and knowledge so far. I have to keep learning and seeking and growing. Each addition of information, each prayer, each story shared from another's faith journey adds new things to ponder. It's exhausting yet exhilarating. When I step back and look at how far I've come knowing God, I realize faith is a lifetime journey. I have come a long way, and we are still together on the road to discovery.

- -

Dear Father, You are beyond measure! I will never know You fully, but there is excitement is learning more and more about You. I want the prize of renewed faith today. Amen

Weighing In

His master replied, "Well done, good and faithful servant!
You have been faithful with a few things;
I will put you in charge of many things.
Come and share in your master's happiness!"

Matthew 25:21

How much yarn am I going to need? How much yarn have I already used? It's a mystery! Well not quite. I learned a trick when I worked at a local yarn shop. You weigh the yarn. I realize this will seem obvious to some knitters and be a big surprise to others. I was in the latter group. It makes perfect sense though; you know a lot when you weigh in. I bought a kitchen scale. I weigh my yarn before, during, and after I knit. Now I can plan and use my yarn wisely.

Last winter I knit a lot of hats for charity. I pulled all kinds of yarn from my stash, using up many great colors and  textures. I worked with a basic beanie pattern. The design fun came by putting different yarn combinations together. And it was easier to plan if I weighed the yarn so I knew how far it would go. I knit one hat in a solid color and weighed it. Then I knew how much yarn I'd need to make a hat that size. Turns out it was 38 grams.

So when I looked at my stash, and pulled out more yarn to play with, I weighed it to see if I had enough for a whole hat. Often times I did not. But I added a few extra color choices and voilà! A whole hat was born. It was great fun to fit together the puzzle of each hat.

Weighing in gives you useful information for all kinds of projects: Do I have enough yarn for the second sock or mitten or glove? How much yarn do I need for this baby sweater? How much yarn did I use for that scarf? I want to knit another one! It helps so much in planning and using resources wisely.

And I love the stewardship of this technique. I use what I have on hand rather then buying more yarn. Most knitters I know have far more yarn then they have time to knit. Sometimes I feel guilty for all the yarn in my stash. But I've found weighing it helps me better use what I already have. What is in your stash that you can use now? Weigh in, and find out.

– –

*Dear Father, I love to buy yarn! I have so many
pretty choices in my stash. I want to be a good
steward of all I have. Remind me to go shopping
in my stash soon. Amen*

Biblical Knitter

She selects wool and flax and works with eager hands. . . .
She is clothed with strength and dignity;
she can laugh at the days to come.

Proverbs 31:13, 25

The woman described in Proverbs 31 gets a bad rap. She is, after all, annoyingly perfect. She cooks and cleans and raises the children. She's wise, faithful, strong, disciplined, and noble. She's a smart businesswoman as well as keeping her husband happy at home. She may even be a size six. It seems she has her whole life effortlessly together. But I wonder, just maybe, if she's able to do all those amazing things not only because she loves the Lord but she also has the good sense to knit.

Verse 13 says: She gathers wool and flax and works with eager hands. She knows she is making fabric to clothe her family. And she also knows she will get a moment's peace when she knits. She will have time to herself to think and dream, pray and plan. I'm sure I'm taking liberties with my interpretation, but isn't it a lovely thought that

God gave this busy woman a way to relax in the midst of her industry?

You and I know this secret of knitting. You and I share the delight of fiber in our fingers. Like the Proverbs 31 woman we are eager to get to our knitting. Even when struggling with a difficult pattern or having made a mess of a project, there is something so satisfying about knitting. In all the things listed that woman accomplishes, it is a happy thing to see knitting called out as a good thing for her to undertake.

I may not measure up to the to-do list sketched out for the Proverbs 31 woman; nonetheless I am a busy woman. I have many responsibilities and find that knitting keeps me sane in the midst of all the demands on my time. So I will gather wool and flax and work with eager hands. I will find a moment's peace and enjoy the gift of knit time in my day. You can do the same. No guilt in knitting—there is peace provided when you work with wool.

- -

Dear Father, the list of virtues for a woman sketched out in Proverbs is overwhelming. I want to measure up but fall short. Remind me of the peace I can find when I take a moment to step back, take a breath, and regroup. Let my eager hands find time to knit today. Amen

The Fabric of Life

*For you created my inmost being; you knit me together in
my mother's womb. I praise you because I am fearfully
and wonderfully made; your works are wonderful,
I know that full well. My frame was not hidden from you
when I was made in the secret place, when I was
woven together in the depths of the earth.*

Psalm 139:13-15

How perfect that the metaphor the psalmist used to
describe God's intimate relationship with us is one
about knitting. It's the very fabric of life! To create each life,
God took our measure and put each detail in place. He knows
each one of us on a cellular level.

Covering a loved one with knitted fabric is an intimate
act. You have to measure their body to make it fit. Baby booties won't fit man feet. Toddler sweaters won't wrap around
Mom's shoulders. Fingerless gloves won't work on baby hands.
What size is your loved one's chest, head, arm, or foot? Those
precise details matter. Get it right, and they will be covered
with warmth and love. Get it wrong, and you'll be re-gifting
someone else with your handiwork.

God got it right. Though I might argue sometimes, I

28

am not tall enough. My hair is not curly enough. My green eyes are fading. Of course, these are all superficial complaints because deep down his work is perfect. It is amazing our bodies work so well. Hearts pump continually. Breath happens without thinking. Joints bending. Food digesting. It's spectacular when you take a moment to consider the intricacies of your body.

Yes, there are those who have serious health struggles, and that is a whole separate life to live. But most of us can take a moment to marvel over how astonishing we are. We walk, talk, sing, dance, drive, think, create. The list of human activity is endless. And one of the things He gave you is a set of hands that loves to knit.

Next time you pick up your needles just watch as your hands make stitches automatically from muscle memory. The eye-hand coordination required is an elegant dance. Then think of your Lord working carefully to knit your body in your mother's womb. You were made with His tender love. He took your measure and knows you intimately.

- -

Dear Father, my body is a marvel! Even when it's
not working as it should, it is an amazing
machine that keeps going and going.
I am astonished. I am grateful.
I am happy to be Your creation. Amen

Tuesday Night Knits

Therefore encourage one another and build each other up,
just as in fact you are doing.

1 Thessalonians 5:11

Carving out time for a weekly meeting is tough when we are all so busy. But there is one meeting I put on my calendar anyway. The first and third Tuesday evenings of each month are blocked off. I guard this time and look forward to it. Those are my knit nights.

Tuesday evening I walk down the street and knock on my friend Anke's door. She always calls out, "Come on in. It's open!" I am expected. As each knitter arrives, Anke calls out again, "Come in!" Soon the room is full of women chatting. We each pull out our work, find our place in a pattern, and start where we left off. We admire each other's progress, we hold up finished projects, and we seek advice through tangles.

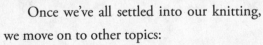

Once we've all settled into our knitting, we move on to other topics:

How is your sister?

Did you finish that book I lent you?

Is your car fixed?

Have you heard about the job interview?

How was that cake recipe?

We share an interest and connection to each life around the circle. Knitting brought us together with a common craft, but caring for each other became a vital part of our gathering as well.

Some weeks Tuesday evening is the only time I make progress on my projects. But more importantly it is a time I treasure to connect with my friends. I know about their cares and concerns, and they know my worries and joys. I am invested in helping them as a sounding board, cheerleader, helpmate, or prayer partner. When there is sadness—a grown child moving cross-country or a long job hunt left unfulfilled—we pray for one another. And when there is joy—a new home, a new baby, a new job—we celebrate together.

Communities of all kinds can feed your heart and soul. You can share more than a common activity, goal, or interest. Knit circles are particularly special. Members share their expertise and fiber opinions, and the happiest circles share their lives with each other too.

- -

Dear Father, thank You for all the communities
I enjoy. It is a joy to travel life together with those
willing to carry my burdens. And give me the strength
I need to carry their struggles as well. Amen

Woolen Prayers

*Carry each other's burdens, and in this way
you will fulfill the law of Christ*

Galatians 6:2

My answer to many of life's highs and lows is to pull out my knitting needles. Baby on the way? Of course I'll knit a blanket, booties, or tiny cardigan for your new little one. Going off to college? I'll make some warm socks for your first winter. New house? Do you want a throw for the family room or tea towels for the kitchen?

I celebrate even smaller occasions. First day of school? Here's a new hat to keep your ears warm on the walk to class. Meeting an old friend for coffee? I bring along a coffee cup cozy for fun. Sometimes I even pop an unexpected gift in the mail to a friend. Here's a scarf to let you know I'm thinking of you today. I can think of all kinds of reasons to share a woolen celebration.

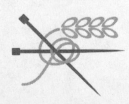

Life's news is not always happy. Those are the times a celebration is not waiting on my needles. Instead there is a need for comfort. Cancer diagnosis. I will knit a very soft hat for you—one you can wear when the harsh cold of chemo gets to you. Sharing that little bit of knitted goodness eases my heart. And it offers physical comfort to the one I am holding in prayer. Lost job. Financial troubles. Sick children. These parts of life need just as much knitted support as the joys.

Sure it's great to be able to offer happy thoughts and warm wishes on the joyful occasion of life's milestones. But when life puts up roadblocks, knitting can help then too. Those are the times knitting gives tangible proof of my love. I know holding a sufferer in prayer is a real way to help, but sometimes I want my prayer to be felt like a hug. And I need the comfort of action. I need to be able to wrap a friend in a woolen prayer.

It's my knitter's secret weapon. All those stitches on the needles—there is a prayer behind each one. I am sending off my love. Here, hold tight and feel its warmth.

Dear Father, I love to pour out my heart in prayer.
It's okay for me to have knitted prayers. They often
add physical warmth to the prayers I bring to Your
throne in petition. Amen

Lifelines

Because of the LORD's great love we are not consumed,
for his compassions never fail.
They are new every morning; great is your faithfulness.
Lamentations 3:22-23

I challenged myself with some lace knitting recently. I finished the 12th row of the pattern repeat. Ah. With every stitch in place I saw the design beginning to emerge. How exciting. I was making lace! Yikes, I was nervous. There are so many things to keep track of with lace. I could easily make a mistake. I couldn't read the stitches well enough to correct a tangle. Time to put in a lifeline.

A lifeline is a trick knitters use to keep from going nuts when making lace. It protects the work. I carefully threaded

a thin piece of scrap yarn on a tapestry needle and slid it through all the stitches on my knitting needle. There, all secure. Now even if I made a mistake (as I inevitably would), I could go back to the portion of my work that was correct. If there was an error, I could take all my stitches off the needles and rip back to the lifeline. The thread would stop the work from unraveling completely. Then I could put my project back on the needles and try again. The lifeline gave me the freedom to proceed with confidence. That little bit of thread would keep my work safe up to that point.

Lifelines are such wonderful things. They are the safety net that let my knitting proceed. I long for such a safety net in my life too. Wouldn't it be great to get a do over? How can I correct an error in my life? What kind of lifeline can I use? I have found one that works pretty well: prayer.

I used to use prayer in crisis mode only. Please help! And I'd complain about any and everything wrong. From waiting in line to pleas for good health, I rushed to prayer. But I have discovered prayer is a lifeline I can put in daily. I can lean on God to hold me safely in His care, and I can proceed through my day with confidence. Even if I make a mistake (as I inevitably will), I know I have a lifeline to rip back to and start again.

– –

Dear Father, You are my lifeline! You hold me in
Your tender care every day in every way.
Remind me today to return to You
if I stray from my work. Amen

What Is It?

Who is like the wise? Who knows the explanation of things?
A person's wisdom brightens their face
and changes its hard appearance.

Ecclesiastes 8:1

I don't get it. Knitting is so boring! It's the same thing over and over. It's complicated. Why on earth do you do it? And wool is so itchy!

Have you ever gotten these comments? I have. I just smile; they come from people who are not going to be converted to knitting. They don't see what I see when I look at a sweater or yarn. I am in love with the possibilities or the construction or the feel. Or any number of other things that make knitting my pastime of choice. All they seem to see is repetitive motion injuries and scratchy wool. These detractors don't know what they are talking about. Knitting is fabulous!

We all have a blind spot though. We can't see what is so amazing about an activity someone else finds enthralling. For example, I don't understand why my husband loves to play with puzzles so much. Here's what I see: It's frustrating. It's time consuming just to break a code or unlock a trick box.

Then what? Where is the fun in banging your head against a problem like that? Here's what my husband sees: The ah-ha moment of solution. The admiration of a clever design. The desire to create carefully crafted wooden puzzles. Hmm, maybe it's like the satisfying moment of completing a sweater? Or the thrill of a lovely new knit pattern. I think I can see his point, a little bit.

My husband teases me about my knitting. There is a knit project sitting next to every comfy chair in our house! True. And there are puzzles stacked on many of our bookshelves. We laugh at each other's collections and passions. But I suspect neither of us really understands the thrill the other one gets from their hobby.

Funny thing though: we both know how important it is. My husband has been the one to discover new knit shops for me. And he makes his own dinner on knit nights so I can go out. I, in turn, wait patiently as he combs through puzzle shops when we travel. And I know if he's down in the base-ment he's woodworking on a new puzzle. We give each other space to pursue what we enjoy.

Giving another room is important. I think one of the reasons I get annoyed with people asking me why on earth I enjoy knitting, is they seem to ask with disdain. As if I am someone who has

lost her mind. It's more fun by far to talk to someone who doesn't get it but is interested in why I do like it. They want to understand. Of course they may never "get it" the way I do, but at least they have some insight into why people knit in the first place.

Trying to understand another offers you so much. It opens you up to new insights and observations. It softens your world and gives you an appreciation for things you never knew much about. It gives you education and can fire your imagination.

- -

Dear Father, the world is filled with all manner of fascinating things. Next time I encounter something strange, let me see the wonder of it and even ask questions to discover more. Amen

Marked by Love

And you also were included in Christ when you heard
the message of truth, the gospel of your salvation.
When you believed, you were marked in him with a seal,
the promised Holy Spirit, who is a deposit guaranteeing
our inheritance until the redemption of those who are
God's possession—to the praise of his glory.

Ephesians 1:13-14

I admire Irish fisherman knit sweaters with their twisting cables and complex stitches: basket weave stitch for an abundant catch, honeycomb stitch to encourage a busy worker, cables for safety and good luck. The tales of these sweaters intrigue me. I read knitters used stitches passed down through generations so eventually towns and regions had special patterns all their own. It was rumored these sweaters could identify a man lost at sea. Should he wash ashore, his sweater marked him. Turns out it's all a bit o' Irish exaggeration.

Fisherman knits did come from Ireland, the Aran Islands, but these garments were the answer to poverty and famine, not regional pride and fisherman identification. And the patterns were handed down a few decades not hundreds of years. In 1891 the Irish government created the Congested District Boards to help islanders cope with unemployment and population growth. Fishing was the only employment and sheep the only animal on the land. The Board encouraged people to knit and sell the garments for a second income. Locals embraced the efforts. A cottage industry was born and grew to worldwide proportions and recognition.

And that legend of identifying a man lost at sea? Well it probably came from a play written at the turn of the 20th century, *Riders of the Sea* by Irish playwright J. M. Synge. In the play a woman recognizes her drowned brother by four dropped stitches in his knitted woolen socks. Not long after the first successful production of the show, some clever marketers saw their opportunity and wove the story into the wool industry. The myth grew that women marked their menfolk for their safety at sea.

I like the original flight of fancy: sweaters marking fishermen with safety and good wishes. It's a lovely thought, a garment created to identify the wearer as one of your own: "This is a cherished member of my family."

I think how I am marked by love too, a precious member of God's family. God has called me His daughter. He loved me, you, and the whole world, enough to want us all to be a member of the family. He has covered us with more than a warm sweater for cold days at sea. He has bought us with His life. We were marked by His love even before we knew Him. And responding to that gift of love is a lifetime challenge.

- -

Dear Father, the gift of being in Your family brings tears to my eyes. Thank You for calling me daughter and wrapping me in Your love. Amen

Threads of History

Day after day, in the temple courts and from house to house,
they never stopped teaching and proclaiming
the good news that Jesus is the Messiah.

Acts 5:42

I watched carefully as I made a knit stitch. It fascinated me how both simple and complicated it is. Simple, pull up a loop of yarn and slip it to the opposite needle. Complex, these interlocking loops made fabric I use to clothe others and myself. When I pick up my needles, I am connected to a long line of history. The first knitted socks were found in ancient Egyptian tombs. Thousands of years ago someone figured out how to make fabric, and we've been practicing it ever since. In fact knitting has not changed very much at all.

I love the thought of being connected to a long line of knitters stretching out behind me and yet urging me on: Keep this craft alive! People have been sharing their skills with each other for generations. What's the big deal?

Well if no one shared these skills, the craft would stagnate and eventually disappear. That would be very sad indeed.

What if those who heard the Good News never shared their story? Never told the glory of Jesus birth? Or the thrill of His resurrection? Sharing the Good News keeps it alive and growing. No one beyond Bethlehem would even know if people didn't share their story. Jesus' ministry in Galilee would have stopped right there if no one told the story. Of course the power of God is behind the story, but we need to use our free will and be brave enough to share it. The story has been told with power and conviction. Millions, no, billions know. We are part of that history. We are part of God's story of love. It's our honor to get to share this with others.

You are a part of the long line of knitters practicing an ancient craft. And you are a part of the Christian lineage as well. The stories have come all the way down to you at this particular time and in this particular place. You are a part of passing on all you know and love. From something as simple as a knit stitch to something as spectacular as the Good News from heaven, you have the story to share.

- -

*Dear Father, history is a rich tapestry, and I am
a thread in its pattern. Give me the courage
to share Your story so others can be a part
of this grand design. Amen*

Raglan Construction

Wise men and women are always learning,
always listening for fresh insights.
Proverbs 18:15 (MSG)

One of the beautiful things about knitting is being able to try on a garment as you work on it. Slip the sock over your heel and see if you are anywhere near the toe decreases. Pull a fingerless glove on your wrist and see if you are ready to start the thumb gusset. This seems kind of obvious, but the fact caught me by surprise. I was making myself a top down raglan-sleeved cardigan. After I finished the body of the sweater, it was time to go back and pick up the sleeves.

Sleeves and I don't get along. It seems I have to make at least three for every sweater I knit. The first one is just a test drive because something always goes wrong. I have to backtrack to get it right. They are usually too long. I try to plan ahead, but it never seems to work. Most patterns I've done call for sleeves knit from the wrist up. The beauty of raglan construction is knitting the sleeves from the shoulder down. I realized this time I could stop before they got too long!

So I slipped my cardigan in progress over my shoulders to check the fit. The first sleeve already hit me in the middle of my upper arm. If I continued with the set of decrease mapped out in the pattern, I'd have orangutan arms once again. But I could stop the madness right now. I adjusted the number of plain rows between decreases. It worked! I was thrilled. I love the journey of making a sweater as much as the next knitter. But ripping back is no fun when you just want to wear a sweater that fits!

Why share a "duh" moment like this? Well here's the thing: Sometimes I get a little cocky about my knitting. I know what I'm doing. I've done it so many times before, right? But this project was a reminder there is always something new to learn. There are more nuances to discover, more tips and tricks to ease my way through a project. So rather than sigh over the fact that I've knit for years and am still learning some basics, I got excited. How cool is it that I have more to find out? My hobby of choice keeps me intrigued.

It's not lost on me that I could apply this lesson to other areas. Lifelong learning is a very good thing. I know all I did was get the sleeves right on my current knit project but what a good reminder to keep my eyes open. What new lessons are there for me to learn? If I watch, what other insights will I pick up? I mature in faith

when I pause to reflect rather than rush on "knowing" what is ahead. I do not have all the knowledge I need to get through life; each day I can find something new to learn. Some days that something new is the knowledge I know so little.

- -

Dear Father, I want to be a lifelong learner. Today give me the passion of a beginner even if I've been working at this for years! Amen

Lessons from My Knit Bag

Finally, brothers and sisters, whatever is true,
whatever is noble, whatever is right, whatever is pure,
whatever is lovely, whatever is admirable—if anything is
excellent or praiseworthy—think about such things.

Philippians 4:8

Having the right tools for the job at hand makes it so much easier to get your work done. My knit bag had gotten cluttered with all kinds of extras. So I cleaned it out the other day. As I reloaded my notions pouch, I looked at each tool with a fresh perspective and discovered they could be essential for more than just knitting. I found a couple life lessons tucked in my knit bag. See what you think.

Scissors. Used for snipping off ends of yarn or trimming up a loose thread. My scissors cut what is no longer needed. Sometimes I need to trim away the excess in my life to see what is really important.

Stitch holders, for holding live stitches to be worked later. There are times I have to leave a task undone to wait for perspective, knowledge, or

patience. Waiting for the right time is better than rushing in and making a mistake.

Measuring tape. Are the pieces I'm knitting coming out the correct size? Taking a moment to see if things are on track will save me a world of headache later. In life, too, stepping back for a moment to assess helps make moving forward easier.

Tapestry needle. Used for sewing knitted pieces together. Fixing a tear in the fabric now will save it from forming a big hole later. Mending broken pieces of my life can be time-consuming work, but the effort can bring such peace.

Crochet hook. I need this to add a decorative trim on a garment I'm making. The pretty little details of life are nice. Giving myself the luxury of some pampering is okay—and makes life a little sweeter.

Just a few knitting tools of the trade, but they sparked some ideas for living. Sometimes attaching new insight or meaning to a tool or object in your day can be a gentle reminder of a lesson learned. Take a look in your notions bag. What do you find?

- -

Dear Father, keep my eyes open today.
There are insights all around me.
Show me a life lesson. Amen

Swatches

Whatever your hands find to do, do it with
all your might, for in the realm of the dead,
where you are going, there is neither working
not planning nor knowledge nor wisdom.

Ecclesiastes 9:10

Gauge matters. Too few stitches per inch and your sweater turns out tiny. And just a half stitch too much every inch makes the sweater too big. Most knit patterns have an instruction in bold print, sometimes even all caps: KNIT A GAUGE SWATCH. IT WILL SAVE YOU TIME LATER. Hmm, true. Yet I have skipped this step countless times. Sometimes I have good reason. I am knitting a sweater for charity, and any size will do. Or I'm making a scarf or blanket where size doesn't matter much. But when I am working on a garment, it's foolish to skip the swatch. If my gauge is off, the sweater won't fit. All my work will be wasted.

Swatches get a bad rap. They are tedious. They are practice. They get discarded. They get unraveled. They take time away from starting the project. All thoughts I have had.

And yet swatches are an essential step in making a sweater.

I've been thinking about the swatch in a different light these days. A swatch is the small, behind-the-scene necessity. It's not glamorous. You can't wear a swatch, but it's a foundation. Get this right, and you are well on your way to a lovely outcome.

How much behind the scenes work am I willing to do? It's more fun to show off a flashy new sweater than to sit and swatch. It's more fun to listen to a great speaker than set up the chairs for everyone to sit in. It's more fun to chat over coffee than get up early to make a pot for everyone. The little acts that happen without much notice are often the very details that make the main event possible.

If you are moaning about the tedium of swatching, think of it as a time spent laying a foundation. Time you are using to ensure the next phase of the project will go well. Stretch this thought just a little and maybe next time you are asked to do something mundane to help another, it will come a little easier. The little things can be essential in ways we don't always appreciate.

— —

Dear Father, mundane is boring. It's hard to enjoy
a behind-the-scenes task. Next time I am asked,
let me step up with the joy of service. Let me be thinking:
"I want to help!" rather than: "I have to help." Amen

Follow the Directions

*You will keep in perfect peace those whose
minds are steadfast, because they trust in you.*

Isaiah 26:3

My friend Susan ripped out her work—again. She was
making cables for the first time. She said they didn't
look right. What she meant was they didn't look like the
picture. "You have to trust the pattern," I told her. "It takes
several rows to see it emerge. For now just be careful to check
your cable turn in the right direction. You will see the effect
once you have enough rows."

A pattern is a comforting thing. All the details are spelled
out, making it easier to see where you are going. Follow the
directions, and it will come out picture perfect, most of the
time. Sometimes, like my friend Susan, I get stuck. The directions instruct me to do something that seems wrong. How is
this supposed to get me to the end product?
Hmmm.

Don't you wish there was a pattern for
how to live life? Just adhere to a prescribed
set of steps and everything will fit perfectly?

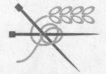

Then even if you were taking the twists and turns of a cable, you could be certain of a lovely outcome. We do have such a pattern for living: God's Word. The Bible reads like an instruction manual showing us how to live. Trouble is I don't always trust the instructions. Sometimes I pick and choose what to follow. This approach doesn't work so well. Picture a pair of socks where you choose not to close the toes. Not very useful.

Listen to some of the instructions the Bible gives us: Love your enemies (Matthew 5:44). The last shall be first (Mark 9:35). Turn the other cheek (Luke 6:29). These do not sound good or easy to do. They offer a complex pattern. What to do? I want the lovely outcome, but it seems hard to achieve.

Thoughtful prayer and further Bible study helps make these directions easier to understand. Even if I find myself still baffled and waiting to see how things will turn out, I have God to lean on. He listens when I bemoan the fact that the pattern is not turning out as I thought it would. Like waiting to see the stitch pattern emerge in my knitting, I have to wait to see what pattern God is making in my life.

- -

Dear Father, give me a glimpse of the pattern You have set out for me. I want to trust You more with the project of my life. Amen

Picture Perfect

For it is by grace you have been saved, through faith—
and this is not from yourselves, it is a gift of God—
not by works, so that no one can boast.

Ephesians 2:8-9

When my husband cooks, he wants the meal to look like the picture in the cookbook. Then he knows it's turned out right. I want the same thing when I knit. I want my project to be picture perfect. I feel like a master knitter if things go well and my project begins to look like the photo. And I am always amazed when it does.

It's turning out like the picture! Sometimes I rush to show my husband. But honestly he just can't get as excited as I do. "Look!" I gush, "it's just like the picture." He is nonchalant. "Of course it's like the photo. That's what you were aiming for, right?" "Yes, true, but don't you see it actually is like the photo!" He doesn't know about the fear I have. It might not work. I might not be able to pull it off. I don't have the right skills. I'm not accomplished enough.

A lot goes into getting my knit project to be picture perfect: the right yarn, an accurate gauge, hours of fussing with the stitch counts, cable turns, shoulder caps, hems, decreases. So many details to get right or have go wrong! So it's a celebration for me when things are going well. I did it!

All this struggling with perfection made me think of the verse about good works verses grace. I still think I can work my way into heaven. If I do all the right things, I will be guaranteed a spot. Just like if I work hard enough my sweater will turn out perfect. But there is no work that needs to be done to get into heaven. Jesus has already done the heavy lifting. There is not a thing we can do.

Faith. Letting in the knowledge of God's saving grace. That is what is required, to see that I am God's own child. And I am already picture perfect in his eyes.

- -

Dear Father, You have covered me with grace and accepted me as Your daughter. Let me live in that holy thought today without struggle. Amen

The Search

Keep my commands and you will live; guard my teachings
as the apple of your eye. Bind them on your fingers;
write them on the tablet of your heart. Say to wisdom,
"You are my sister," and to insight, "You are my relative."

Proverbs 7:2-4

Hunting through knit patterns is great fun. There are so many sites online as well as books to flip through. And if you are a member of the Ravelry website, you might be like me: able to lose hours clicking through the thousands of choices there. It is fun to dream of all the knit possibilities. I often begin the hunt for one pattern, and others pop up to entice me as well. I make note of them all. Of course I will never have enough time to knit everything I want to try. But the thrill of the hunt is great fun. I like the research.

The same sort of hunting and research can happen with bible verses.

I am always a little in awe of people who know the chapter and verse of what they want to find in the Bible. They can call up a verse from memory. I've heard

the Bible stories and studied the verses for a lifetime, but I do not have lots of verses memorized word for word. And I certainly don't have their addresses in my head. It is not a discipline I possess.

I remember a time when I was depressed and struggling to find my way back to trusting God. A dear friend suggested I turn to the Bible for comfort and instruction. I knew that was a good idea but had no thought where to start. I wanted a quick fix of comfort. She suggested I look in a concordance to find my way. "Start with the word *trust* and see where it takes you." What a help to find a reference that could point me to the topics I needed most. I read verse after verse. Over time I found my way back to a place of trust in God.

I discovered using research materials is a little like looking at knit patterns; other interesting things catch my eye. Soon I am investigating other verses and trains of thought. Though I still can't keep verse addresses in my head, more comfort and insights into God's Word comes to me as I study and that is the gift I seek.

- -

Dear Father, digging into Your Word brings me the comfort I seek. Finding a new way to investigate Your Word is an exciting way to keep it fresh in my mind. I appreciate the resources of research. Amen

Monkey Mind

He says, "Be still and know that I am God;
I will be exalted among the nations,
I will be exalted in the earth."

Psalm 46:10

When I knit I find peace. I feel calm. It is a time I can rest. Though my fingers are moving, my mind is slowing down. I love the quiet place knitting opens in me because sometimes I suffer from monkey mind. You know what I mean: thoughts crashing into one another or swinging in from every angle. The loud chatter of insistent problems. The repetitive loops of to-do lists that won't be quiet.

My mind churns when I worry too much or feel overwhelmed with too many things to do. I can't settle. There is no focus to my thinking. I often reach for my knitting needles when this happens. It is a sure way to calm my mind and maybe find a way out of my troubles. I even creep out of bed some nights when I can't fall asleep. I knit a few rows, and then I can go back to sleep.

Sometimes I feel guilty for picking up my knitting. This is a selfish waste of time;

I have things I have to do. But I pause and devote my thinking to a few rows. My brain gets quiet as I concentrate on my work. I hone my focus to this one simple task and shut out all the rest.

Knitting quiets my mind so I can think. So I can pray. So I can find my way back to a peaceful way of being. This is when knitting is my lifeline not my past time. This is when knitting is the calm waterfall in the middle of the monkey mind Amazon. And this is when I am quiet enough to hear from God. Knitting slows my thoughts enough so there is room for peace to step in and space for me to feel a nudge from God. If I am quiet, I can hear what He has to say.

It's like that commercial from the 1970s for Coty's Nuance perfume: If you want to capture someone's attention, whisper. I have to be quiet to really listen. Straining to hear makes what I find all that more important. When the noise in my head is too much, when I want quiet, I pick up my knitting. I usually find the calm I was looking for. Here is a space to be still and listen to whatever God wants to say.

- -

Dear Father, I am trying to quiet my racing
thoughts so I can hear from You.
Help me find the peace I seek. Amen

The LYS (Local Yarn Shop)

*Then he said to them all: "Whoever wants to be
my disciple must deny themselves and take up
their cross daily and follow me."*

Luke 9:23

Running a yarn shop takes more than warm and fuzzy feelings. It even takes more than a love of yarn and knowledge of knitting. It takes some business savvy. That's the hard part to remember, turning a profit to keep the doors open. I have worked in several yarn shops over the years. I've watched as owners juggle expectations and more to try and stay in business.

Knitters and crocheters are lovely people. They are pleasant customers and enthusiastic artists. So running a local yarn shop (LYS) can be great fun. There are cool benefits. You get to order all kinds of yarn. You can contact knit celebrities and invite them to your shop. You get to go to trade shows to hunt for the latest notions and sample the latest yarns, and hear about the hottest trends. But you have to order what your customers will buy. Each shop caters to a

specific clientele. You don't get to buy just what excites you as the shop owner. You must know your customers and be on the look out for exciting things to entice them. Knitting is a great hobby, but when you turn it into a business there is even more work to be done.

I have been thinking of how running a yarn shop is like the business of living a Christian life. It may look all warm and fuzzy on the outside, but on the inside it is work. As a Christian, you can have the warm feeling of growing in faith with Jesus in your heart. But if you "take up your cross daily," there is a responsibility of work to be done. It may be a clear road to follow but not always an easy one. Sometimes that feeling (God in your heart) nudges you to go out and do a hard and difficult thing. Maybe you will be called to forgive or to serve or to act in ways outside your comfort zone. Or, equally as difficult, you will be called to stay within and do the hard work of maturing your faith, maybe through study or prayer.

Running a yarn shop involves budgets, rent, utilities, payroll, and a long list of other responsibilities. It's not all pretty new yarn and great new patterns. It is labor to keep the doors open, but the rewards can be great. Over the years a shop can become a hub of community activity as well as a source of pride and income.

Prayer, study, service these are a few of the things to keep our Christian life vibrant. It takes work to stay connected to our faith, but the reward is great. We believe in nothing less than eternal life. We are saved by the God of the universe. Yet sometimes it feels easy to slack off and walk away from God and His nudges in our heart. But like having a thriving business, the work in our heart pays off. Our connection to God makes our life glow with His Spirit. We have partnership that lasts a lifetime.

Dear Father, I am walking the road of faith together with You today. I call on Your strength to help me continue to grow. I look to You for the guidance to attend to all the tasks You have set for me to complete. I know You are with me. Amen

Fresh Eyes

"I will refresh the weary and satisfy the faint."
At this I awoke and looked around.
My sleep had been pleasant to me.

Jeremiah 31:25-26

There is a rule in my house: No Knitting after 10:00 PM. At the very least I have to switch to a simple garter stitch project. (Knit every row.) Too many times I have been working along only to discover a dropped stitch, a miss turned cable, or a bungled increase late in the evening. It's a bummer of course. I should put my work away right then. Stop. Rest. Yet I often dive in and start to fix whatever is wrong.

The problem is late at night I am tired and should be winding down, not trouble-shooting knit mistakes. I often would compound the problem, dropping more stitches or slipping the work off the needles to rip back all the rows I'd just completed. Or even worse, "fixing" something that was never even a problem in the first place. Fatigue. It's time to stop! Eventually I'd give up in frustration. "I'll attack this problem in the morning." And attack was what I wanted to do!

Here's why my rule came to be: I discovered in the morning I could easily fix what was wrong. For one thing I could see what was wrong. I was calm and had more patience with my work and myself. I came to the problem with fresh eyes.

Taking a breath and being gentle with myself is not easy. I love to knit. Why not keep going and going for hours of fun? Well sometimes, as every knitter knows, there are hours of frustration. It's just string and sticks; how can they get the better of me? Was I cocky? Was I lazy? Was I just tired and not concentrating? All of the above.

The morning brings perspective. Fresh eyes and a rested brain help to untangle the mess I made. Sometimes the "mess" is an inaccurate stitch count. I thought I'd dropped one when it's tucked right there on the needles safe and sound.

Rest and patience. My knitting is teaching me these are just as important as progress and industry. But what I really want from my hobby is calmness and enjoyment. Coming to my project with fresh eyes I can have fun rather than frustration.

No Knitting after 10:00! It's for your own good.

- -

Dear Father, remind me that balancing work
with times of rest is important. Give me patience
with myself so I will stop and recharge
when I should. Amen

The Selfish Knitter

So then, just as you received Christ Jesus as Lord,
continue to live your lives in him,
rooted and built up in him, strengthened in faith
as you were taught, and overflowing with thankfulness.

Colossians 2:6-7

I have knit a lot of sweaters, many of them for myself. In fact, stop me before I knit myself another green sweater! One of my knit friends describes this kind of knitting as selfish. She describes herself as a selfish knitter too. I asked her what she meant.

"Oh I only knit sweaters for me!"

"Really? Never a hat for someone else? A scarf for a friend? A sweater for a new baby?"

"Well of course—sometimes—but most often I fall in love with some yarn or a pattern and I make it for me."

I started wondering if I was a selfish knitter. It seemed like a bad thing the way she described it. I looked for warning signs. I saw a few:

I guard my knit time, grabbing a few rows every day.

I hunt patterns for the next great sweater I want to wear. I have enough hand-knit sweaters to wear a different one every day for a week.

I buy tons of sock yarn and only wear hand-knit socks in the winter.

I am a selfish knitter! I think my friend described her knitting as selfish because of who received the finished product. I think of selfish knitting not as who receives the garment but who gets the benefit. And I get the benefit, big time! And this is not a bad thing at all. I looked at my knit habits in a different way.

I knit because I need to. Having fiber in my hands is the calmest way for me to be. All the craziness in my head is quiet when I can sit with needles and pattern. This is not selfish. This is a way to slow down and find some peace in my day. It's my quiet time.

I chat with God while knitting. Prayer seems too strong a word for just hanging out in His lovely presence while I have fiber in my hands. I do bring my thoughts to Him, but more often than not it's a time when I say thank You for a hobby that brings me such peace and joy.

Yes, I am selfish in wanting more knit time. Just one more row is the excuse I use. I'll stop after the next pattern repeat or the next color change. But it's the calm and quiet knitting brings I really want to prolong.

I am a selfish knitter. I love this hobby. The discipline of slowing down forces me to get quiet. I know when I'm knitting may be the only moment God can get my attention. I'll be selfish for that any day!

- -

Dear Father, I find joy in Your presence.
And knitting keeps me quiet enough to find You in
the busyness of my life. I love it when You join me
for some stitch time. Amen

Yarn Overs

Many are the plans in a person's heart,
but it is the LORD's purpose that prevails.

Proverbs 19:21

A yarn over makes a hole on purpose. As a beginner you probably made several yarn overs and considered them mistakes, not realizing they are a technique to learn. It's called a yarn over because you literally pass the yarn over the needle without working it. It creates both an extra stitch and a hole.

Some yarn overs are part of the pattern. Others appear and are a problem. That is when you need to pause. You have to assess what you have done and figure out how to remedy the mistake. It might mean asking for help.

Sometimes I think God is making yarn overs in my life. He's poking a hole in my plans. I might be working toward a particular outcome or goal, and it's not turning out as I envisioned. I thought I knew what I was doing, but look at this hole! It's a mess I need to address. Taking the time to honestly look at my plans sometimes I find they are not God's plans. We need to make a pattern correction together.

God poked a hole in what I was doing to change the pattern, to get my attention. It's time for me to follow His lead or at least respond to His nudge to change direction. This is unsettling and makes me feel uncertain. I don't like it. How did I get so far off track? Rather than beat myself up for too long, I try to pick up my work and find a way forward. A new pattern may emerge in the fabric. This will be a piece we work on together.

A change of plans is painful. And sometimes I make things even worse by picking apart details trying to fix it. I see a repair is needed, and I rush to correct, only to find I have created a bigger problem. I realize I did not sit for a minute to figure out what the best fix would be. What is it God wants me to do?

Changing direction is not easy. Ripping out my work is hard. It can take a long time to see that yarn-over hole as a good thing, a place where God put His finger on my work and made it His own again. But when I yield and follow His pattern, we are working together toward His plan.

- -

Dear Father, correction is difficult.
I balk at Your discipline. Help me align
my plans with Yours. Help me see the wisdom
of the pattern correction. Amen

Gifts to Share

Each of you should use whatever gift you have received
to serve others, as faithful stewards of
God's grace in its various forms.

1 Peter 4:10

Sometimes I latch onto a project and knit it over and over just for the fun of it. Coffee cup cozies was one such pattern. I was noodling around with cable ideas. I wanted to perfect my skills and got carried away. I started experimenting with different cables. I loved to watch the twists unfold. And these cozies were so little I could play around with lots of different turns. Some designs failed, but a few were just right. And the little project was a great way to use up stash yarn. Pretty soon I had four-dozen cozies! Crazy I know.

It was such an easy project to take along. A bit of yarn, an index card with the pattern, and off I'd go. By the time I got back from a train ride into the city or a wait at the doctor's office, I had a new little gift. And that is what they started to be. I handed out cozies all the time. I sent them to family. I gave them away at

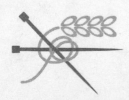

my knit circle. I brought them along for friends when we went out for coffee.

Knitting just for the fun of it gives me the pleasure of sharing my creations with others. And this bit of whimsy does not need to fit; it was always the right size! How sweet to make someone smile with a surprise. It is a small amount of my time and talent but a huge return in smiles and happiness.

Sometimes knitting feels like a hobby just for me, a tiny thing that gives my pleasure. But knitting is a gift I can share in so many ways. It's a talent given to me from God, and I in turn am charged to share it with others in all kinds of ways. I can hand out a coffee cozy. I can knit in the community of friends. I can help others with their knit projects. I can knit for charity. I can even pray while I'm making stitches. This gift gives me so much pleasure. It's a joy to have so many ways to share it with others. No good gift is small. It's how we use it that makes it big.

- -

Dear Father, I love knitting. I have such fun
making things. I enjoy sharing what I make.
Thank You for giving me a heart that is happiest
when knitting to share. Amen

Metal Or Bamboo

When you said, "Seek my face," my heart said to you,
"Oh LORD, I will seek your face."

Psalm 27:8 (GW)

What kind of needles should I use for my project? There is so much to consider when answering this question. For one thing knitting requires many different sizes of needles. US size 1 is needed with fingering weight yarn to make a pair of socks. US size 8 will give you a nice cardigan working on worsted wool. And if you want to work big and fast, US size 15 yields a lovely, bulky cowl to keep you warm in the winter.

And size is not the only variable to consider when selecting needles. What are your needles going to be made of? Do you want to work on metal? Plastic? Bamboo? Do you need straights, circulars, or double pointed? And budget. What price can you afford? You can find lovely hardwood needles for as much as $35 a pair. Oh my. Decisions. Decisions. Metal needles will let the yarn slide easily, but if you are working with a slippery linen fiber they will be too slick. Circular needles can hold far more stitches than

straight needles. Making a blanket is easier if you have room for all your work rather than cramming it on a needle that is too short. Which needles are best for your project depends on all these factors as well as your personal preference.

Double-pointed bamboo needles will knit up a lovely sock. So will two plastic circular needles. And don't forget some of us like to use the magic loop method with one really long cable on our circular metal needle. Once the sock is complete, is there any way to tell how it was produced? Hmm. No. Not really. The sock looks the same.

How many different ways are there to approach God in prayer? More ways than there are knitting needles. Sitting quietly is the image that comes to mind. Yet there are lots of ways to pray. Some use the meditative comfort of a rosary. Some write thoughts out in a prayer journal. Some go away on retreat. Some offer service as prayer, or artworks or music. You can sit quietly or praise loudly. You can be inside or outside. How we pray is not as important as the prayer itself. And what do we bring to God in prayer? Sometimes we come running with joy, excited to share our love for God. Sometimes we come with tears, hoping God will take the hurt away fast. There are as many ways to engage in prayer as there are people praying.

We each have a unique way of entering God's presence. There is no one right way to do it. Pray aloud. Pray long. Pray in short desperation. God will listen to it all. Coming into His presence is what counts. He is delighted you came whether you leapt in His lap with joy or you crawled to the base of the throne with a heavy heart. Being with Him is the part that matters, not how you got there or what kind of prayer you offer. Prayer is not about making sure you use the right words. Prayer is engaging heart to heart with God.

- -

Dear Father, I am seeking You in prayer. I come in joy. I come in sorrow. I come. I come with the confidence knowing You are always there to catch me and listen. Amen

Bundled Up

*If we confess our sins, he is faithful and just
and will forgive us our sins and purify us
from all unrighteousness.*

1 John 1:9

I set out for a walk on a crisp autumn morning bundled up in my favorite wool sweater. I pulled a soft hat over my ears. I wrapped my neck with a lovely wool scarf. I slid my hands through a cozy pair of fingerless gloves. And my toes were toasty in some hand-knit socks.

As I walked, the engine of my body began to heat up. So I adjusted my temperature. I started to shed my layers. I loosened my scarf then unwound it completely. I pulled off my gloves then tucked them in my pocket. I yanked the hat off my head. I unbuttoned my sweater. It was a nuisance to carry all my stuff while I was walking. How convenient it

would be to leave my things at the side of the trail. What a release, to walk unencumbered.

I thought of the other layers I am bundled in. I am wrapped in faith, draped with love, and covered with creativity. And I am also bound by pride, tied with resentment, and constricted with anger and envy. I need to peel off some of these layers. If only it were as easy to let my pride slip through my fingers, as it is to slide the gloves off my hands.

The release my body feels from the extra layers of clothes is the same release my soul craves from my sins. I have already been given the permission and forgiveness to toss all my sins aside and walk free in Christ. Jesus gave me that freedom when He died for me. I am the one still clinging to ugly burdens and unnecessary layers. It is hard to loosen my grip on comfortable trappings. I cling to my familiar ways, but I work up a sweat and feel pressed to change.

It is my prayer to strip off one layer and break free. Change one way of wrapping myself in burdens I don't need. This will take time. I am sure I will offer this plea to God again. But today I am going to try and loosen the bond of one heavy layer and claim my forgiveness.

- -

Dear Father, help me unwrap one sin today.
Help me find a way to forgive myself for
holding onto something that is hurting me.
Let me choose Your forgiveness. Amen

Multitasking

Cast all your anxiety on him because he cares for you.

1 Peter 5:7

AT THE SAME TIME. These are directions that strike fear in the heart of this knitter. This means I will have to follow multiple directions simultaneously! Sometimes it gets overwhelming. For example: shaping underarms, shoulders, and neckline while following three separate cable charts. So much to keep track of. How can I figure this all out? One row at a time. Concentrate. Take the next step. Don't look too far ahead, but stay focused on what is at hand.

Sometimes we pride ourselves on multitasking. Don't we? We try to get so much done all at once. Maybe we can, or maybe we are fooling ourselves. It would be better to attend to one thing and do it well rather than squeeze in too much and do a poor job of everything. There is something to be said for

attention. For taking our time to lean into the task at hand and give it our all! Besides doing things AT THE SAME TIME is hard!

Why do we multitask anyway? There is some kind of "glory" attached to being the person who gets a lot done. I am trying not to be that person anymore. That is not glory; it's exhaustion. When I do one thing at a time, I finish a job more quickly and can move onto the next thing. Yes sometimes my to-do list stretches out, and I don't get to everything I want to accomplish in a day or a week. But the important things always seem to get finished.

When I am still and focused, when I allow myself to concentrate on one thing at a time, I can take pride in the task completed. I get into it. Writing daily, doing errands, cleaning the house. There is a long list of to-dos for me. Not everything on the list is great fun. I don't like to "attend" to laundry, but it does get done every week.

Here's the thing: I don't think God made us to accomplish a long to-do list each day. I think He made us to live in His world and help each other out. He didn't make us to feel anxious about all we need to do. He made us to be loved and take the time to love. I don't love laundry, but I love the ones I am keeping clean and clothed. It's a subtle shift in my thinking, but it slows me down and I try to do one thing at a time. Multitasking is my enemy. I try to single out one task at a time and do it well.

- -

Dear Father, show me the one task that needs doing today. Save me from multitasking my time into uselessness. Give me the joy of one job well done. Amen

Happy Hobbies

Every good and perfect gift is from above,
coming down from the Father of the heavenly lights,
who does not change like shifting shadows.
He chose to give us birth through the word of truth,
that we might be a kind of firstfruits of all he created.

James 1:17-18

When I start counting my blessings the usual nice things came to mind. My health is good. My family is fine. My basic needs are being met in sufficient ways. Hooray! I am a blessed daughter of God. But honestly, I take much of that for granted. Sigh. So I paused and looked for something I'd probably forgotten to say thank You for.

I am grateful I have a hobby. I knit every day; it's my "thing." It is creative work I love to do. Knitting fulfills me in a way little else can. The colors of yarn, the feel of fibers, the multitude of patterns, the endless list of people I want to knit for—it all makes me very happy.

And there is the knit community. So many lovely people enjoy this same hobby. Every week I go to a knit circle. I get to play with my knit peeps. We invade our local Starbucks. There we sit for two hours chatting and knitting. We share our projects and our lives. Every week I watch the progress of their knitting and they see mine, but we also check in with each other. We cheer news about vacation plans and job changes, and we support one another through hard moves and painful losses.

Knitting also offers me time alone. In the morning quiet or late afternoon, I can grab my needles for a few rows. The stress of the day melts; I become settled and calm. The needles clicking and the stitches slipping back and forth, it's soothing. I have plenty of time alone to enjoy it. And knitting time opens up the freedom to reflect.

If knitting is this important to me and I get this much pleasure from it, it has to be a gift. Not just the wooly gifts I make for others but the very activity itself. Knitting is a gift to me. When God was handing out blessings, we each got our own unique collections of goodies. Hobbies abound.

I happen to love knitting, but I can't sew on a machine at all. My sister-in-law is a whiz with her sewing machine; her hobby is quilting. My brother is a baker. My father-in-law is a glass artist. My brother-in-law is a banjo-playing bluegrass musician. My husband collects and designs wooden trick puzzles. My cousin is a photographer. My mom is a beader. My aunt is a reader. Each one of us has a hobby we love. These hobbies offer each of us more than just a way to pass the time. We find a community of others who enjoy our passion. We find creative outlets to express who we are. None of us is making any money at these pursuits. Nor are we turning them into businesses. We are doing our "thing." We are just enjoying our gifts.

Next time you begin to count your blessings (and I highly recommend doing this sometime very soon), think of all the little ways God has enriched your life beyond the basic needs to keep you alive. I bet you find joy in places you might have never thought to look.

- -

Dear Father, thank You! Thank You for caring enough about the joy of play to give us so many activities to choose from and enjoy. Thank You for tailor-made creative ways to have fun. Amen

The Learning Curve

Whoever gives heed to instruction prospers,
and blessed is the one who trusts in the LORD.

Proverbs 16:20

Do you remember your first knitted project? I can vividly picture the orange creation I made. I learned to knit at the local library. They offered a class for kids, and I was eager to sign up. My mom was a knitter. She'd offered to teach me of course, but I was a headstrong teenage daughter not interested in letting her help me. So when this class came up, we both jumped at the chance for a neutral instructor.

The project was a stuffed snake. Just what every young girl wants, right, a reptile she can display on her bed. I guess the snake was a step up from a scarf since we had to learn to increase and decrease, tapering the ends of our work so there would be a head and a tail. We also learned how to sew it together to make a tube.

I was not a patient student. I got frustrated easily—one reason Mom was reluctant to teach me I think. I wanted to have the clean easy movements I saw in the teacher. The learning curve seemed steep. I would never have the grace she did!

To her credit the teacher was a patient woman and showed me over and over how to cast on.

I struggled to make a few stitches. Is this right? Ack, there's a hole. I have the wrong number of stitches. I don't see how it works. My list of complaints stretched on and on. I didn't give myself any leniency. I pushed. I was stubborn. I will get the hang of this.

Then I made the mistake of comparing my work to others, noting they seemed to have no trouble at all slipping stitches from one needle to the other. The work grew on their needles. My work was a messy inch or two of struggle. I fought with my needles and yarn. I didn't want to climb the learning curve; I wanted to vault over it!

I practiced at home. I knit every day. And then something happened. I picked up my work one afternoon, and it felt right in my hands. I seemed to know what I was doing. I produced

a whole row without complaint. I saw the flow of making stitches, and it felt lovely. A switch flipped. I had climbed the learning curve and was sliding down the other side.

They say practice makes perfect. I say practice lets a skill become ingrained. Practicing the knit stitch made it automatic—eventually. I still run into techniques and stitches I have no idea how to do. Now I realize it takes time to learn a new skill. I give myself room to learn rather than jump to frustration. Patience while we are learning is a gift we can give ourselves.

- -

Dear Father, learning a new skill takes more patience than I have sometimes. Grant me the peace of knowing perseverance will pay off in my next new endeavor. Amen

Knitting Lesson

Blessed are those who mourn,
for they will be comforted.
Blessed are the meek
for they will inherit the earth.

Matthew 5:4-5

When I worked in a yarn shop, I helped knitters through their trouble spots all the time. I showed some how to cast on and others how to bind off. I found dropped stitches. I sorted out next pattern steps. I was pretty confident I could detangle most simple knit problems. Then Marlene walked in.

Marlene did amazing crochet work. She could make a baby sweater in two or three days. I can barely chain a crochet edging on a piece of knitting. But now Marlene was learning to knit. She had been working on her first pair of socks for a month. It was time to close the toe. She needed help.

 Grafting the toes together calls for a scary part of knitting: the Kitchener stitch. I've made lots of socks. When I close the toe I need a quiet room. I have my Kitchener cheat sheet to

guide me. If I loose my focus in the middle, I start over. Could I really teach someone else?

Marlene was a patient student. She was gentle with herself, taking notes and taking her time. She listened and was not afraid to ask questions. I was the nervous teacher, not confident in my skills. But it was a slow time in the shop, and we had the place to ourselves.

First I wrote out the directions for the Kitchener stitch. I was amazed I could remember it by heart. Then I sat beside Marlene. I took the first stitch. Oops, you learn by doing not by sitting beside someone. I handed over her sock. I read off the directions as she followed along. We sat, heads together, easing the stitches of her sock into place and closing the toe. We took our time. We laughed a lot.

As we worked Marlene told me she was all alone. She had recently lost her mom, daughter, and uncle. Marlene knit and crocheted to keep her mind and heart busy. She had a job, but time alone in the evenings was tough. She said needlework saved her.

At last we completed the 14 stitches at the end of her sock. We were both so proud of the outcome. We grinned at each other. We had each conquered something difficult. She finished her sock. I gained confidence as a teacher. I was petrified when Marlene asked me to help her. But step by step we did it.

It seems like such a small thing to teach a knit technique. Yet Marlene and I shared a laugh and enjoyed each other's company. And we both learned something. She can sew her socks closed, but I got more out of the afternoon. I spent time with a gentle woman. I was reminded to go easy on myself, just as Marlene does. And I rejoiced in the power knitting has to console the lonely and fill a heart.

- -

Dear Father, You comfort Your children in
so many ways. You give us confidence when
we are lacking, and You hold us in Your
tender hands when we are lonely. I rejoice You
care so deeply for each one of us. Amen

Mistakes

Teach me, and I will be quiet;
show me where I have been wrong.

Job 6:24

If you knit, you will make mistakes. It doesn't matter how accomplished you are; sometimes knitting is tricky and you get it wrong. Those are the times you might fall into the five stages of mourning.

5. Anger. I see it. I missed a stitch four rows back. I was so careful! I checked the pattern over and over. But I was knitting on automatic pilot and there it is, a mistake in my work. I could scream with frustration. I have that sick feeling in the pit of my stomach. Stupid, complicated knitting.

4. Denial. Is it really a mistake? It's not that noticeable, is it? I can look right past it and not see it. I think I'll just knit some more and see if it goes away.

3. Bargaining. Okay, it's a mistake. I see it every time I get to the end of the row. Now I have more rows to pull out if I want to correct this stupid thing. Why did I keep going? (Denial, see above.) Maybe I don't

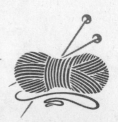

have to unravel the whole thing. What if I try covering it up with a decorative applique stitch or a plan to put a patch on it? What if I put it on the back? What if…

2. Depression. I have to fix this. I see it every time I pick up the project. I can't miss it. In fact, it's all I see. But I hate to rip back. All that time lost! (Anger, see above.) I am such a lousy knitter. (Try not to be too hard on yourself at this stage.)

1. Acceptance. Yup, there's a mistake. I have to fix it. But I might make it even worse. Time to ask for help. (Don't let asking for help make you angry, or the cycle could begin all over again!)

All pretty silly, right? I made a mistake. Big deal. It's not rocket science; it's knitting. There are no knit police coming to take me away. I can fix this. And asking for help is sometimes the hardest part. However, guess what, my expertise grows when I make a mistake. I have learned so much from other knitters when I humbled myself enough to ask for help.

- -

Dear Father, I find it hard to be humble and
ask for help. Remind me I learn more when
I ask questions then when I struggle alone. Amen

Novelty Yarns

Let the message of Christ dwell among you richly
as you teach and admonish one another with all wisdom
through psalms, hymns, and songs from the Spirit,
singing to God with gratitude in your hearts.

Colossians 3:16

I can be a yarn snob. Oh I don't use novelty yarns. I don't use man-made fibers. I am a purist. But sometimes, I get seduced. Beads and bangles. Feathers and frills. Novelty yarns bring unexpected surprises to my knitting. For the sheer delight of it, it's great to play with something crazy: wild colors, unique fibers, even wire! Breaking out of the wool box is kind of fun. It stretches me because being a purist limits my possibilities.

I put limits on other things as well. For example, I like my worship in church to sound a certain way. Music is a hot-button issue in many churches, and the debate will continue. But let me say there are many ways to express our joy. I like what I grew up with, of course, the hymns of a Catholic mass. Yet I've been equally

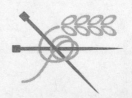

moved to tears listening to guitar or jazz piano offer music in a service. And sometimes a drum set is just what you need to really shout to the Lord. Both traditional and contemporary are heartfelt worship. I don't want to limit my expressions of praise just because I am stuck in my thinking.

Novelty yarns have a place in my stash. They are the bits I pull out when I want to explore silliness or experiment. But I shake my head when I knit with beads and sparkles; I am just not a fussy kind of gal. And besides, remember that yarn snob thing? I am a little embarrassed when I knit with bling. Yet sometimes those are the very fibers that make my project pop.

Contemporary music has a place in my worship. It allows me to think in new and different ways while honoring God. It makes me uncomfortable to have such a raucous celebration sometimes, but when my heart is swelling with praise, it is perfect way to say I love You, Lord!

There is no one right fiber to use when you knit. And there is no one right music to use when you praise God. All the choices are allowed. And you can use any one in the moment that gives you the best path to praise.

- -

Dear Father, free my thinking today. Let me
celebrate diversity and embrace the variety of
expressions we can use to praise You. Amen

Don't Help Me

Be wise in the way you act toward outsiders;
make the most of every opportunity. Let your conversation
be always full of grace, seasoned with salt,
so that you may know how to answer anyone.

Colossians 4:5-6

The Baby Surprise Jacket (BSJ) is an iconic knitting pattern. Elizabeth Zimmerman created it in the 1930s. It's still popular today. As simple as the stitching is, it still can be intimidating to knit. There is lots of counting, and it looks like an amoeba while you are working on it. The surprise comes in the end; you fold the fabric and with just one seam, ta-da!, a baby sweater. Great. However even picking out yarn for this project is tough; you can use just about any yarn you want, thin or thick, solid or variegated. Each choice creates a different look and size.

The yarn shop where I worked was offering a class to make the BSJ. Knitters came in to get their supplies for the Saturday class. A customer asked me to help her pick out some yarn.

"Do you have a color in mind?"

"Not really."

"Would you like it to be for a newborn or a toddler?"

"Just show me some yarn."

"Well it could be this." I pointed to some sock yarn. She picked up a skein. "Or you might like this." And I reached for some worsted weight yarn.

"Just tell me what I need!" I started to reach for another yarn. "You know what I don't have time for this, and you are not helping." She tossed the skeins in my hands and rushed out of the store. I stared after her. So strange. I wanted to help. I felt bad that I couldn't find the supplies she needed.

At the end of my shift, the phone rang. "Hello this is Lisa. How can I help you?"

"Have you been in the shop all day?"

"Yes I have."

"Well I owe you an apology. I am the lady who was trying to pick out yarn for the class this weekend. I'm afraid I was very rude. It had been a bad morning. I was very hungry. I shouldn't have yelled at you like I did." Oh my.

"How nice of you to call and say something. I really appreciate it. If you have a minute I can tell you why the BSJ is such a moving target when picking out yarn." We talked for a couple minutes, and she promised to come in the next day to select supplies for the baby sweater.

When I am wrong and I need to sincerely make amends for my actions, I need prayer for the strength to act in a kind way. An apology will be long remembered. That angry knitter yelled at me years ago, and I still remember the relief of knowing I had not caused her such distress. I know it took courage for her to call.

— —

Dear Father, saying I'm sorry is so hard.
I have to admit I was wrong. I have to be humble,
and I have to truly want to ask for forgiveness.
If I need to apologize to someone, please give me
the strength to do it—today. Amen

Goldilocks

Let them give thanks to the LORD for his unfailing love
and his wonderful deeds for mankind, for he satisfies
the thirsty and fills the hungry with good things.

Psalm 107:8-9

Too much? Too little? Or just right? It all depends on your perspective. Five minutes: too long to hold your breath but not enough time to drive across town. Five dollars: too much to pay for a candy bar but not enough to buy a stock investment. Five hundred feet: too far to throw a baseball but not far enough to land a plane. Five balls of yarn: too much to knit a pair of mittens but not enough for a blanket.

Perspective is important. Sometimes you have abundance, and sometimes you have deficiency. And like Goldilocks we would rather have things be "just right." I have been thinking a lot about this and wondering how it feels when I am wishing for God to be more present in my life.

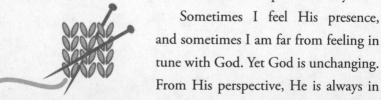

Sometimes I feel His presence, and sometimes I am far from feeling in tune with God. Yet God is unchanging. From His perspective, He is always in the same position: caring for His child. I am the one who wants the "just right" feeling. I don't want to have to wait on God. I want His answers right now. Yet I don't want too much of God either; I want the freedom to do things my way.

Hitting the sweet spot of living a life with God takes a lifetime of trying. When I am in tune with where God wants me to be, I move through my days with a sense of purpose and peace. And when I am far from His presence, I spend time wishing He'd save me from boredom, or stress, or fear, or loss, or any bad thing in my life. Then I long for more of His presence. But I also fear feeling smothered. Even when I have known the sweet spot of trusting God with my days, I fall back to wondering: *Can I trust Him to be in control?* But I have discovered He has plans and ideas and ways for me to be that I never would have thought up! I never thought I'd travel to Japan or live in New York or be a published author. However all those things have come to pass.

I don't think God puts us in situations we are not built for. He puts us in places that are just right for us. I will probably not be going to Africa on a mission trip, but I will be asked to live my faith in my own neighborhood. I will probably not be asked to teach college, but I will be asked to share my life lessons with those I meet in my day-to-day world. I will probably not be asked to drive a formula one race car, but I will be asked to take a neighbor to a doctor's appointment.

The sweet spot in life then is keeping in touch with God. Finding Him in prayer. Waiting on Him with patience. Loving Him with praise. From my perspective that is "just right."

- -

Dear Father, Goldilocks and I want that just right feeling. Remove my anxious thoughts so I can understand being in Your presence is the just right place I need. Then I can wait with patience, praise with joy, and work with peace. Amen

Full-Sized Love

*Dear friend, I pray that you may enjoy good health
and that all may go well with you,
even as your soul is getting along well.*

3 John 1:2

I have knit dozens of sweaters for charity and many for friends having babies. I have a growing collection of sweaters I knit for myself. And I have knit lots of little things as well: hats, scarves, cowls, and socks. I've even made some stuffed animals. But to get a full-sized, grown-up sweater out of me, you pretty much have to be a blood relative. Making a sweater is such an undertaking, I want the person I knit for to have a vested interest. I want to know they will wear it.

For several years I picked a family member to give a sweater for Christmas. Long about July I'd tell them it was their turn. I would show them a few different patterns I would enjoy knitting and I thought they would like wearing. Once we settled on a design, I took careful measurements; I wanted this creation to fit. Finally we would go yarn shopping. Matching a color and yarn they

like to one that is perfect for the project is a tricky thing. I was surprised one year when my purple-loving sister-in-law picked out a lovely shade of turquoise blue for her cabled hoodie. Who knew?

Once I have all the materials, the real fun begins and I don't mean the casting on. I mean I start sending the recipient updates of sweater progress: *I've finished the back! Gosh, I wonder if I'll make it by Christmas? The front was tricky but a good challenge.* It was fun to tease the person about my progress without showing them the sweater. It's silly I know, even a little mean, but a way for me to let them know I was working on their gift and thinking of them too.

Whatever I make while I am knitting, I think of the person who is going to get the work of my hands. Not for every single stitch, but every time I pick up the project I have the recipient in mind. Even if I am knitting a tiny hat for a preemie infant I will never meet, I pray for the child: Please keep this child safe, help her to grow, give her parents peace in their new role. Prayer infuses my knit time with meaning and reminds me I am knitting with love and not just wool.

When Christmas finally arrives, I present a new sweater to my loved one. They have heard about it but not seen it. It's a special moment for both of us, kind of a shared secret all year. Even with all my careful planning, sometimes things still don't turn out right. One year I had to rework sleeves that were too long. However there is no doubt of the love behind the needles. All my prayers for the person weren't wasted. In fact, prayer is probably the most important part of the sweater. I wrapped my loved one in prayer all year long.

– –

Dear Father, I want to wrap people in Your love.
I want them to feel Your presence in their lives.
Let my hand knits be a tangible way to deliver my
love and prayers to the world. Amen

Comfort for the Furry

In his hand is the life of every creature
and the breath of all mankind.

Job 12:10

When I started knitting for charity, the usual ideas came to mind: chemo caps for cancer patients, sweaters for kids in need, blankets and scarves for the homeless. All kinds of people needed knitted goodness to keep them warm, to let them know they were loved. It never occurred to me that furry creatures needed any of my handicrafts. I was wrong.

At knit night one of my buddies cast on a very bulky yarn. I was surprised; that's not usually her yarn of choice.

"What are you making?"

"This will be a cat mat. I can finish one in an evening. They are so quick."

"How many cat mats do you really need? You only have one kitty."

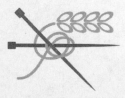

She giggled, "I know, but the SPCA has dozens of kitties in need."

Turns out our local Society for the Prevention of Cruelty to Animals, and many others around the country, was in need of blankets for cats. The kitties wait in metal cages, spacious enough but still a cage, to be adopted. Small and frightened, sometimes never having known kindness, these animals wait for a new family to find them. A cozy place to rest is nice.

Knitting a little mat 18 inches by 24 inches is a quick thing. These mats are also the perfect project to start kids knitting for charity. It is simple and not so large they give up. You can even knit for a particular cat at the shelter if you like. (It may be hard not to adopt after that!) This project also eats up the scraps of yarn in your stash.

Once a cat is adopted to a new home, the blanket goes with them as a transition piece. It is something familiar during a big life change. If you have a soft spot for cats, this is a nice way to share your knitting with the furry. Check with your local SPCA for their needs and measurements for the project.

It's a comfort to knit for an animal in need. When you consider charity knitting, think of all God's creatures, not just the ones who can say thank you.

- -

Dear Father, even kitties need love and kindness.
I am happy to share my knitting skills to bring
comfort to the furry. Amen

Superpowers

Just as a body, though one, has many parts,
but all its many parts form one body, so it is with Christ.
For we were all baptized by one Spirit so as to form
one body—whether Jews or Gentiles, slave or free—
and we were all given the one Spirit to drink.
Even so the body is not made up of one part but of many.

1 Corinthians 12:12-14

The average hand-knit sweater contains thousands of stitches. They are not all alike. There are dozens of choices for casting on and hundreds of choices for the main stitch patterns. As simple as stockinette: knit a row, purl a row. Or as complex as a combination of increases, decreases, yarn overs, and other fancy moves. Binding off, too, presents more choices. One garment, many stitches.

And the finished project should be a wearable garment. That is our chief aim as knitters, right? All those different stitches come together to make a sweater someone can wear. If we cast on endlessly, we have nothing but a needle full of yarn. And if we knit rows endlessly, we'd end up with a piece of fabric so big no one could wear it. The trick is putting the parts together to make a whole.

There is variety of purpose to the stitches we take. And there is a variety of work to be done in the world. We each have different jobs and areas of expertise. Yet sometimes I feel my offerings are not as important as another's. I compare my small contributions and fret I am not making a mark, or doing enough. I don't give myself enough credit. You might get caught in this trap too. Wishing you had different, better, or more gifts to offer the world's needs. The truth is we each have a superpower all our own, that special something only we can give.

If knitters only made lace, our toes would be freezing for want of warm socks. If we only got to use the garter stitch, we'd never have the beauty of cables. Taking one item out of the knitting library leaves a hole to be filled. Keeping your gifts to yourself deprives the world of something special it needs. Use your superpower today. Big or small, it's just what the world needs now: your love!

- -

Dear Father, You have given each of us work to do.
And our roles in this world are integrated.
Every task needs to be addressed. Remind me to
play my role with enthusiasm. Amen

Knit for Marie

Honor your father and your mother,
so that you may live long in the land
the LORD your God is giving you.

Exodus 20:12

I knit more things for my mother-in-law then I ever realized. There's the green shawl she asked me to make her when we saw a sample in that cute little knit shop in Santa Barbara. There are the denim blue socks she picked out the yarn for in Estes Park. There is the cowl I made to go with her purple ski jacket. There is the Pearl Buck jacket I knit for her out of dark turquoise one year for Christmas. And there is the black and blue shawl I knit for her to keep warm the winter she was battling cancer.

I know the specific list of these items because I recently got them all back. My dear mother-in-law passed away. As

my father-in-law was cleaning out, he didn't want these hand knits to go into the Goodwill box. I am happy-sad to have these things returned. I'm sad because they remind me of the lovely woman who isn't here to wear them anymore, but I'm happy she enjoyed them so much.

She liked to show off her kids. She bragged about my husband and his two sisters often. They are all three accomplished. They did well in school, chose good mates, made lovely homes, and have fulfilling work. She was proud of me, too, and counted me as one of her kids. I knit her some love, and she wore it with pleasure, letting others know who made it for her.

Rather than tuck these special pieces away, I pull them out and wear them myself now and then. I miss her. I'd love to call her on the phone and catch up. She was great for a long phone conversation. The next best thing is being wrapped in one of the knit pieces and thinking of her. She is as close as possible then.

You may never get back any of the beautiful things you've knit for loved ones over the years; however, that is no reason to quit sharing your craft. You are lucky enough to know how to say I love you with yarn. Let this be your reason to pick up stitches and wrap someone you care for in a woolen hug.

- -

Dear Father, I am reminded of all the garments I have knit
for family and friends. These are garments I have created
to give warmth and comfort for years and years. It is a blessing
to give and receive these tangible reminders of a love. Amen

Baby Sweaters

The king will answer them, "I can guarantee this truth:
Whatever you did for one of my brothers or sisters,
no matter how unimportant they seemed, you did for me."

Matthew 25:40 (GW)

The announcement of a new baby coming excites most knitters. Oh goodie, tiny baby things to make! Favorite patterns are pulled out. Yarn is purchased. Love is cast on the needles. And if the new little one is a new grandbaby or niece or nephew, there is even more joy. Our family is growing, and the next generation is coming.

I wonder if Jesus' grandmother was thinking that way? Were his aunts excited about His birth? There was so much mystery surrounding His birth. There was probably some concern, maybe even some unkind discussions. They probably did not think they would be welcoming a king. Not every baby enters the world with joy. Some babies need extra love and help.

None of my friends needs baby items these days. And the kids in my family are not old enough to have kids of their own yet. When I knit for family members, I am making garments for big people, but I love to cast on little things. To fill my need for delighting a new mommy and baby, I knit for charity. I know there is a child just the right size.

Knit for Kids is my charity of choice (KnitForKids.org). They are a division of World Vision. They send sweaters around the world to children who need a bit of love and warmth. I love to knit for them. I choose any color. I make any size. I know the sweater will fit; there is a need for every size and color. I have fun knitting. Sometimes I put in crazy colors and bold patterns on the simple pattern from their website. I want the child who gets my sweater to have a bright spot of color and know there is joy behind the sweater they are wearing.

I think of the child I will never meet as I knit. Wondering where they live and praying they get more help than just a warm sweater. Every baby deserves a warm welcome to this world, but not every child receives that luxury. My knitting needles can provide such a gift. It is a privilege to knit for them.

- -

Dear Father, I want to help new babies with love and warmth. I want them to have a start that knows You. May my charity knitting bring some comfort to a new little one. Amen

Heating Up and Making Changes

Not only so, but we also glory in our sufferings,
because we know that suffering produces perseverance;
perseverance, character; and character, hope.
And hope does not put us to shame,
because God's love has been poured out into
our hearts through the Holy Spirit, who has been given to us.

Romans 5:3-5

Wet felting is when you dunk a piece of knitting in the washing machine on a hot cycle—heating it up, adding friction so something new and stronger emerges. You shrink your knitting—on purpose! What started out as a large loose piece of work becomes a tight, new creation.

Felting is not an exact science. The outcome is not assured. There are lots of variables. The finished size may be very different from the original. And then again, it may not 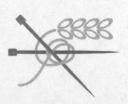 even change at all. If you use the wrong yarn, nothing happens. One hundred percent wool felts the best. Synthetics do not alter state. Acrylic contains too much man-made fiber so it resists the process.

We want it to shrink. We want it to become a firm, sturdy fabric. Some felting is so strong it can hold water!

Felting can also take a long time to happen. First you take the time to knit a large piece, then you get it wet and add friction. Agitating the fabric to make it stronger can take hours. The work has to be worn down to make it solid. The water makes the wool fibers bloom. Then they can grab onto one another and bond while being spun around. And as anyone who has been surprised by a tiny wool sweater coming out of the washing machine knows, the procedure cannot be undone. Once wool is shrunk, it stays that way.

The felting process is an apt metaphor for life changes. Think about it. In felting you start with a large amount of natural material, and through heat and friction you shrink it to a sturdy new creation. Compare this to a big life change. There's a lot of material (questions, worries, doubts, fears) to shift through. Then things heat up. There is agitation as you struggle to find your way through the changes. But eventually you are on the other side of the change, a different person than you were before, hopefully stronger. Even happy changes like the birth of a child cause worry. Life will never be the same. It will be different, yes, but will it be better? Can I handle this?

I know I resist the friction of change. Especially when I am not sure of a positive outcome. What value does this transition have for me? It is then when prayer and trust become essential. I have to believe God is helping make me stronger, that the changes happening in my life have value. I will be a new creation in Him and for Him. Philippians 4:13 says, "I can do everything through him who gives me strength." And there is my comfort. I am being changed for the good with strength He provides.

– –

Dear Father, change heats up my anxiety levels.
I feel rubbed the wrong way. Remind me I am
moving toward a stronger faith. I am gaining a
stronger life in You. Amen

Nature's Patterns

*What has been will be again, what has been done
will be done again; there is nothing new under the sun.
Is there anything of which one can say,
"Look! This is something new"?
It was here already, long ago; it was here before our time.*

Ecclesiastes 1:9-10

I love to look out the window when I'm flying. It's not a perspective I get to see every day. There are so many cool patterns when I look down. Farmland squares. Mountain peaks. Lakes. Deserts. Even city streets and houses are in patterns. It's the natural motifs I marvel over though.

Last winter when I flew cross-country several times, I looked out on miles of white, but even then there were unexpected designs to find. We flew over frozen lakes. The deep water in the middle was not frozen solid so it stayed blue-green while the shallow shores were crystals of light blue. It sparked my imagination. I envisioned some of my favorite knitting patterns. I realized how many of them are taken from nature. I looked at the landscape a little

differently. Smiling, I saw lace shawls and cardigan edges. I thought of mitten backs and pullover fronts. No wonder designers get so much inspiration from nature.

Each designer and knitter puts her own spin on a project. You may be saying to yourself, Yeah, but I'm not a designer. Wait a minute; the very act of picking a particular pattern and pairing it with your particular yarn choice makes the project unique to you. It's true there is nothing new under the sun and knitting fads spread through the community with great speed, but we each bring that one thing no one else can: our unique vision. The creative spark in you is a gift from God. You can use it for all kinds of good things. Whether you knit for charity or grandkids or your own wardrobe, you have the spark of newness on your needles. You share in the creation of something new every time you pick up your project and put the next row of stitches in place.

- -

Dear Father God, I love all the patterns in our
world, from rippling waves to flowering petals.
There are so many places to find inspiration.
Thank You for the gift of creativity. Just working
a pattern takes creative effort. Amen

Weaving in the Ends

Get up! It's your duty to take action.
We are with you, so be strong and take action.
Ezra 10:4 (GW)

I often knit with a solid color of yarn, fewer ends to weave in that way. Color work leaves tons of threads to anchor. I try to weave in the ends as I go, but that is a discipline I don't always follow. Inevitably I get to the end of project and have lots of threads to tuck in. Bummer.

This is a tedious part of knitting. It's even worse than knitting a gauge swatch. I love to wear a project or give a knitted gift, but the details of finishing can be a drag. Yet those very details make the item useful. If you never bind off, your work is stuck on the needles. If you never close the toes, you can't wear the socks. If you never seam the sweater, it's just flat pieces.

It takes discipline to finish a project. The fact that I have so many works in progress should tell you something. I love to start! I'm always on the lookout for new things to knit. But finishing? That takes commitment.

Yes, I have finished a lot of things, but I grumble. Or worse, I race through

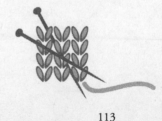

the end bits just to get to the next beginning. Taking time to finish well means using self-control. I am so close! I want to see my results NOW. Paying attention to all the details of the work makes the whole piece beautiful. I pray for the calm and the determination to pay attention to all the details, to take my time, and finish well.

Of course I'm not talking just about a sweater I can wear. I am thinking of other times I rush through something wanting to get to the end and move on. Have I lost my interest in a conversation when I should focus on my friend? I have missed the opportunity to listen well. Did I brush aside a request for help because I knew it would take time to fulfill? I have missed an opportunity to serve.

We've all heard the devil is in the details. He certainly is. He is the one making me complacent when I should be focused on the little things that are important—taking time to listen, to serve, to weave in my ends! These are all small yet significant tasks. I need practice in doing these things. First I'm going to have to slow down and pay attention to the details.

- -

Dear Father, what details am I overlooking?
Slow me down and give me eyes to see the little
things that are so important today. With joy,
let me take action where needed. Amen

Knit Your Bit

Be joyful in hope, patient in affliction,
faithful in prayer. Share with the Lord's people
who are in need. Practice hospitality.

Romans 12:12-13

In World Wars I and II, knitters were called upon to outfit the fighting men in the United States military. The Red Cross had patterns aplenty for knitters to make socks, helmet liners, hot-water bottle covers, scarves, and even plain old bandages. The need for woolens was as great as the need for ammunition. Slogans got knitters to join the war effort: Knit Your Bit, Make Do and Mend, Our Boys Need Sox, Knitting for Tommy. These were rally cries for those on the home front to support the soldiers in battle. Thankfully the World Wars are over, but still countless people are in war-torn places or in the midst of natural disasters and in great need. There are still numerous places where your knitting can go to make a big difference.

Knitting for charities is a very satisfying way to spend your knit time. I have one knitter friend who tithes her stitching time. Each week she spends one day knitting only on charity projects. She makes lots of scarves for the homeless as well as countless baby hats for preemies. I like to knit my bit for the World Vision Knit for Kids Project. (KnitForKids.org.) I feel good about sending sweaters to children who would otherwise not have a warm garment. And knitting my donation is a personal way to offer comfort rather than buying clothing from a store.

Maybe you have a charity of choice too. If not, there are many to choose from. A quick search on Google will give you lots of ideas. You might even feel the urge to start your own charity effort. I encourage you to find an outlet for your knitting energies and even tithe your knit time. We no longer have posters and banners urging us Our Boys Need Sox, but there are a lot of folks who could use your handiwork. Finding a way to share your hand-knits benefits both sides of the needle. You will find a pleasure in helping others not to mention busting your stash down to size. And recipients will have a new sweater or hat or scarf made just for them.

Soothing the hurt of another with yarn may seem like a small thing, but it will make a big difference to that person. The verse in Romans tells us to help those in need. It goes even further; we are to "Be devoted to one another in love. Honor one another above yourselves" (Romans 12:10). That little bit of knitting will go a long way to let someone know they are cared for and loved. I hope you can cast on some warmth soon. Knitting is a gift of compassion within your power to offer.

- -

Dear Father, let me see where my knitting is needed. Plant in me the seed to want to spend some of my knit time working for those who are less fortunate than me Amen

Progress on the Needles

*But you, dear friends, by building yourselves up in
your most holy faith and praying in the Holy Spirit,
keep yourselves in God's love as you wait for the mercy of
our Lord Jesus Christ to bring you to eternal life.*

Jude 1:20-21

It's fun to watch a project grow and change on my needles. The start is exciting: casting on, counting stitches, and setting up patterns. Any addition in the beginning is visible immediately. But in the middle of the project, it's harder to see progress. Especially if I am working on a cabled sweater or complex lace pattern, it can take hours to do just a few rows. Is there any progress? I check often to give myself encouragement. In fact, sometimes I put a stitch marker in my work when I start knitting for the day, just so when I finish I can see I made a difference. I changed something, and hopefully for the better.

I look for progress in my faith life as well. My faith started when I was a little girl; I have no great conversion story. I was told about Jesus as a child, and my faith has matured over time. I've been through big highs like marriage, childbirth, and retreats that recharge my faith journey. And I've been through big lows such as relatives dying, serious illnesses, and major cross-country moves that all pushed and tested my faith. Of course those events all shaped my faith in strong ways. But when I look for growth, I usually look for small things.

I think it is the daily and weekly practices that keep me connected to my faith journey—the discipline of daily devotional readings and weekly Bible study. The habit of writing notes of encouragement to friends. The desire to keep prayer central to my relationship with God. Like the next row in the pattern I am knitting, my faith progresses one day at a time. Small things help me build a big strong faith.

Take a look at one small aspect of your faith, and see where you too are making progress toward a big strong faith. Put a marker in today and watch for growth; it's coming.

- -

Dear Father, the little things I do daily
to keep the faith are the big things that connect
me to You. Strengthen my resolve to keep
my faith practices in place. Amen

Darn It!

Because the Lord disciplines the one he loves,
and he chastens everyone he accepts as his son.
Endure hardship as discipline;
God is treating you as his children.
For what children are not disciplined by their father?

Hebrews 12:6-7

I hate ripping back, but it's part of knitting. Still, undoing several inches of work bugs me. The lost time! But more than that, I am annoyed with myself for making the mistake in the first place. I'm better than this!

I fell in love with a heavily cabled pullover. I always wanted to try a fisherman's knit. And I figured my knitting skills were finally up to the task. So I cast on. The pattern

required following three separate cable charts at the same time. I grabbed sticky notes to hold my place in each chart. I checked each cable turn to make sure I flipped it in the right direction. Settling into a rhythm I got confident. This is going so well. Look at all my progress. I'll have this finished by the end of the month.

I knit for hours and stopped checking every cable turn. Then I held up my knitting to admire my inches of completed work. Oh no! There was a mistake. And it was a big one. Five cables running up the back of the sweater all twisted in the wrong direction. I put the work down and pouted. Darn it! Now it's ruined. How could this happen to me? I followed the charts. I knew what I was doing! Frustrated, I threw the sweater in my knit bag and pulled out a pair of socks to work on instead.

The wise knitter realizes she does not know everything. Mistakes will happen. She knows she will learn from each project she attempts. The smug knitter rushes forward and does not work thoughtfully. She places blame. The pattern was poorly written. The yarn. The needles. The lighting. There are lots of scapegoats for her troubles. It's still hard for either knitter to rip back.

Clarity comes with the morning. I took my sweater project out of the bag the next day. Assessing the problem I determined I needed to pull the work off the needles and rip back two inches. By doing this I lost my place in the charts. But I slipped the work back on the needles and began to look for clues to figure out where I was in the pattern. Counting cable stitches is difficult. I couldn't find my place. Then I realized if I counted my rows in the plain section of the pattern I could figure out where I was.

It's hard to admit when I am wrong. I hate to be corrected; it's annoying and embarrassing. It's one thing to rip back a knitting project, but it's another thing to correct a life mistake. Have I wronged someone? Do I need to fix an injustice? Is it my job to apologize first? Sometimes, yes, it's God telling me to take a situation off the needles and correct my mistake. Calming down from my frustration brings the clear head I need to fix the problem. Humbling myself to backtrack shows me a better way to move forward.

Dear Father, continue to correct me.
I know working on my imperfections will take
a lifetime, and I also know I will grow in maturity
and faith with Your leading. Amen

Thanks, Mom

Start children off on the way they should go,
and even when they are old they will not turn from it.

Proverbs 22:6

My mom knit a coat for me when I was a toddler. She made a special sweater for my first day of kindergarten. She knit matching sweaters for my sister and me one Easter. She knit a doggie sweater for my brother and kitty sweaters for my sister and me. She is very handy with needle and yarn.

Mom has been through all kinds of handicrafts. She had fun with ceramics, tole painting, decoupage, smocking, tatting, needlepoint, and cross-stitch. She landed on beading as her favorite craft years ago and designs an annual Christmas ornament. Before Mom had kidlets (her word), she was a kindergarten teacher. So we got to do all kinds of cool things at home. Finger-painting with toddlers did not scare her.

I got my love of crafting from my mom. I even went into the design field, working as a graphic designer for years (though before the computer age). I've always been crafty. I took up

knitting again when my son was born. I really got into it. Mom admired my work but stuck to her beading projects.

Then one summer I was visiting and wanted to check out a new yarn shop in town. Mom went along for the ride, of course. She got hooked again. There are so many cool yarns these days. She picked out a skein of red (her favorite color) cashmere. *Won't this make a soft scarf? Indeed it will.* And so it began. Mom returned to knitting.

It was fun to share this craft with her as an adult. The weird thing was I showed her how to do some things. Of course she remembered how to knit, but some of the tips I had learned were new to her. We enjoyed knitting together again.

My mom gave me a love of crafting. I'm happy she took the time to share her passions with me and teach me how to do many of the things she could do.

- -

Dear Father, thank You for the people in my life
who share their passions with me.
They have enriched my life so very much. Amen

Wise Women

Be shepherds of God's flock that is under your care,
watching over them—not because you must, but because
you are willing, as God wants you to be; not pursuing
dishonest gain, but eager to serve; not lording it over those
entrusted to you but being examples to the flock.
And when the Chief Shepherd appears, you will receive
the crown of glory that will never fade away.

1 Peter 5:2-4

Knitting should be shared, and I don't mean just the end product. The best way of learning how to knit happens side by side with the touch of another's hand. Wise knitters share their knowledge of the craft. And a wise novice seeks out an experienced mentor. Sometimes you are the teacher, and sometimes you are the student. Knitting lets you play each role as your skills grow.

Even if you have been knitting for years, there always seems to be another tidbit to figure out or some challenge to attempt. Maybe you want to tackle something intimidating like steeking: cutting your knitting

on purpose! You will definitely need a guide. Or maybe you are the knitter who can show a beginner how to bind off. Sharing this craft is one of the lovely benefits of practicing it. You might be the one discovering a new technique, or you might be the one quietly at work and listening to another person's story. Not all knitting instruction is about the stitches we create. Sometimes it's wisdom from another's life you gain. Knitting provides a place for both those things to happen. And a smart knitter takes a lesson whenever it is given, whether a new trick with her needles or some sage wisdom about living.

I have several knowledgeable knitters in my life. Sure I get answers to my knitting problems from them, but there is so much more. These are women who will give me insightful guidance, or emotional support, or cooking advice, or just a good laugh. I love having older women in my life. In fact I want to be them when I grow up, wise and insightful, or just plain smart enough to know I'm still learning.

My knit knowledge has grown so I can be helpful to others when they are stuck. Yet when it comes to giving out life wisdom, I am a little hesitant. I am still figuring out life. It's true what they say: the more you know the more you realize you don't know that much. Maybe that's the wise part, knowing I don't have all the answers but sharing any small measure of wisdom I do have with a humble heart.

Whether I am offering knitting expertise or sharing my faith, there are gentle ways to share my instruction. I know the lessons that have stuck with me often came in quiet ways. I try to do the same. If I barge in and insist on someone doing things my way, I'm not giving anything they will want to take. Instead I present my insights with love so others will be more willing to listen.

Dear Father, whatever age I am I have skills
to offer. Help me to be willing to be
an eager student as well as a mentor.
Help me find the time and courage to share
my knowledge when it's needed. Amen

I Speak Knittish

*Now the whole world had one language
and a common speech.*

Genesis 11:1

Like many knitters, I travel with several projects going at a time. It keeps me smiling when there are travel delays and fills the time on long flights or waiting to board the next train. I have pulled my knitting out on a long bus ride from Tokyo to a little village where we would explore a woodcarver's studio. I have taken out my knitting on an extended train trip from Oslo to a tiny town in the hills of Norway to see my great-grandfather's hometown. And I've sat in Grand Central Station waiting for the next train to take me home to the suburbs.

Every time, someone approaches me to start a conversation. Sometimes it's a curious person who doesn't knit but remembers their aunt/grandma/mother/  sister knitting, and they want to smile and say how fond they are of watching the craft. But most often another knitter stops to chat. They want to know

what I have on the needles, or where did I get the pattern—
or, Oh they wished they had remembered to travel with
their knitting!

What I love most about these encounters is when the
person checking out my knitting does not speak English.
Gestures tell me she is a knitter. Her smile tells me she loves
the craft as much as I do. Once I had a non-English speaker
direct me to a knit shop I'd missed right around the corner!
It's astonishing to me we can communicate with no words.
It's delightful to share a craft that bridges the need for lots of
discussion. We both speak knittish after all and that's enough.

I wonder if my Christian good intentions are as obvious
as my knitting. Can anyone walking by tell just by looking at
me that I am a Christ follower? It's probably not as immediately apparent as the yarn in my hands. I have to take action
for the evidence to shine. Remember the old song, "They will
know we are Christians by our love"? It is my hope that I live
with a love that is as visible as my knitting.

- -

Dear Father God, I love bridging the gap with
knitting. Thank You, Lord, for the communication
of a smile! May these encounters nudge me
to love the world as You love. Amen

Passion!

*So I commend the enjoyment of life, because
there is nothing better for a person under the sun
than to eat drink and be glad.
Then joy will accompany them in their toil all
the days of the life God has given then under the sun.*

Ecclesiastes 8:15

There is no end to the silliness knitters can invent: jester hats, stuffed squirrels, and even skeleton sweaters. There is also no end to the complex creations knitters can produce: richly cabled sweaters, intricate lace shawls, and elaborate intarsia mittens. Knitting offers hours of entertainment and joy. And that can be all knitting is, a personal joy. If you never knit an item for charity or make a garment to give to a friend, your knitting still has great value: it makes you happy.

I love everything about knitting. Adding books to my knit library. Visiting new yarn shops. Purchasing yarn for my next project. It all gives me such a delight. To a non-knitter this craft can look like a selfish, solitary pursuit. But it is a gift. Knitting is my passion and makes me a happy person. I smile just thinking about my knit time, my next project, or the person getting my knitted item.

That smile lingers and infuses all my time. I can go about my other work with a pleasant attitude. I am a better wife, mother, and worker when I have a positive outlook. And I'm positive my knitting keeps me going. I love this hobby. When I have to leave my needles to do my chores and other work, that's okay; the fun is waiting for me. It's like having a delicious secret, a private way to lift my mood and bring myself joy. I'm content when I'm knitting.

So here is praise to this passion we share. It brings hours of joy, and that in itself is worth thanksgiving. Thank You, Lord, for providing an activity just for the joy of doing it!

What a gift to know we have a God who is concerned with all the aspects of our lives. Yes He cares about our basic needs to be safe, clothed, fed, and sheltered. But He loves us so much He wants us to find joy too. He's given us time and activities for fun and creativity, just to see us smile and play.

Dear Father, thank You for providing for all my needs: food, shelter, and clothing, as well as work and play. You have orchestrated a balance in my life. You know I need rest from work and have given me creative ways to relax. Thank You. Amen

Full Slouch   *Folded Over*

The Slouchy Beehive Hat

This hat is named because it looks like a beehive when completed.

Pattern Notes:
- The purls ridges will be dominant so choose that as your main color.
- Do Not Break the yarn after each color change every four rows; instead carry it up from the rounds below being careful not to pull it too tight.
- Any variegated colors will do. I have found it works out better if you pick a yarn that has very long color changes. The purl ridges are then individual colors, and it looks like you put a lot of work into it when really the yarn did it for you!

Gauge 5 sts/inch

Materials:
- Two colors of worsted weight yarn, at least 133 yards (50 grams) of each (main color and contrasting color)
- 16" US7 needles and US7 DPNs

Instructions:

Using main color, CO 80 sts adult size (CO 60 sts child size).

Join work in the round, being careful not to twist stitches.

Place marker for the beginning of the round.

Purl 4 rounds with main color (makes one large purl ridge).

Knit 4 rounds with contrasting color.

Repeat these 8 rounds, alternating colors until you have

12 purl ridges (you will have just ended with 4 knit rows).

Purl next 4 rounds (you now have 13 large purl ridges).

Next set of knit rounds begin decreasing as follows:

(changing to DPNs when necessary and maintaining

    alternate colors)

Round 1 *K8, K2tog* repeat to end of round

Round 2 Knit

Round 3 *K7, K2tog* repeat to end of round

Round 4 Knit

Round 5 *P6, P2tog* repeat to end of round

Round 6 Purl

Round 7 *P5, P2tog* repeat to end of round

Round 8 Purl

Round 9 *K4, K2tog* repeat to end of round

Round 10 Knit

Round 11 *K3, K2tog* repeat to end of round

Round 12 Knit

Round 13 *P2, P2tog* repeat to end of round

Round 14 Purl

Round 15 *P1, P2tog* repeat to end of round

Round 16 Purl

Round 17 *P2tog* repeat to end of round

Cut 10" tail thread onto a tapestry needle and pull the end through all remaining stitches; secure end by weave in. Share and enjoy.

Cozy #1

Cozy #2

Cozy #3

Coffee Cup Cozies

You can make some cozies of your own. Here are the patterns. These cozies come in three levels of difficulty. From beginner learning to cable through more advanced double twists, you will be a cabling master!

Materials for any one cozy:
- 15 grams worsted weight yarn
  Lighter-colored yarn helps show off the cabling
- US 7 needles, either straights or 16" circular
- Cable needle
- Tapestry needle

Cable stitch abbreviations explained:

CF4 Cable front four: slip two stitches onto cable needle, hold in front of work, knit next two stitches, then knit the two stitches from the cable needle.

CB4 Cable back four: slip two stitches onto cable needle, hold in back of work, knit next two stitches, then knit the two stitches from the cable needle.

COZY #1
SINGLE TWISTS
(Beginner)

This design creates two side-by-side cables. The cables are made in one row and all turn in the same direction, making it easier to remember.

Instructions:

CO 19 sts

Row 1: [K4, P1] 3 times, K4
Row 2: K5, P4, K1, P4, K5
Row 3: [K4, P1] 3 times, K4
Row 4: K5, P4, K1, P4, K5
Row 5: K4, P1, CF4, P1, CF4, P1, K4
Row 6: K5, P4, K1, P4, K5

Repeat rows 1-6 eight more times or till work measures 8 to 8.5 inches

Bind off. Sew seam. Weave in ends. Slip on a cup. Enjoy your coffee!

COZY #2
FRONT & BACK PRACTICE
(Intermediate)

The cabling goes in opposite directions in this design but still only happens in one row, number five.

Instructions:
CO 18 sts

Row 1: K4, P1, K8, P1, K4
Row 2: K5, P8, K5
Row 3: K4, P1, K8, P1, K4
Row 4: K5, P8, K5
Row 5: K4, P1, CB4, CF4, P1, K4
Row 6: K5, P8, K5

Repeat rows 1-6 eight more times or till work measures 8 to 8.5 inches

Bind off. Sew seam. Weave in ends. Slip on a cup. Enjoy your coffee!

COZY #3
CIRCLES OF CABLE
(Advanced)

Now the cabling goes in both directions and happens in two rows, numbers three and seven. Take your time and pay attention to which direction you are headed.

Instructions:

CO 18 sts

Row 1: K4, P1, K8, P1, K4
Row 2: K5, P8, K5
Row 3: K4, P1, CB4, CF4, P1, K4
Row 4: K5, P8, K5
Row 5: K4, P1, K8, P1, K4
Row 6: K5, P8, K5
Row 7: K4, P1, CF4, CB4, P1, K4
Row 8: K5, P8, K5

Repeat rows 1-8 eight more times or till work measures 8 to 8.5 inches

Bind off. Sew seam. Weave in ends. Slip on a cup. Enjoy your coffee!

About the Author

As both a gifted writer and accomplished knitter, Lisa Bogart practices both of her passions every day. She has gifted over 70 sweaters to *Guideposts'* Knit for Kids. Her award-winning devotions have appeared in several publications, including *Guideposts*, and she is the author of *Come on In: Taking the Hassle Out of Hospitality* and *Knit with Love, Stories to Warm a Knitter's Heart.* She lives outside of New York City.

You can visit Lisa online at LisaBogart.com

- -

If you would like to knit a sweater for a child in need, you can go to this website: KnitForKids.org. It will delight your heart to cast on one of these simple gifts of love.

IF YOU ENJOYED THIS BOOK, WILL YOU CONSIDER SHARING THE MESSAGE WITH OTHERS?

Mention the book in a blog post or through Facebook, Twitter, Pinterest, or upload a picture through Instagram.

Recommend this book to those in your small group, book club, workplace, and classes.

Head over to facebook.com/LisaBogartAuthor, "LIKE" the page, and post a comment as to what you enjoyed the most.

Tweet "I recommend reading #KnitPurlPray by Lisa Bogart // @worthypub"

Pick up a copy for someone you know who would be challenged and encouraged by this message.

Write a book review online.

WORTHY®
PUBLISHING

Visit us at worthypublishing.com

twitter.com/worthypub

worthypub.tumblr.com

facebook.com/worthypublishing

pinterest.com/worthypub

instagram.com/worthypub

youtube.com/worthypublishing